CW01021331

Best wishes for
Christmas 91 Dad
with love from
John, Pam, Marcus & Julian

BLUEJACKETS AND BOXERS

BLUEJACKETS AND BOXERS

Australia's naval expedition to the Boxer uprising

BOB NICHOLLS

ALLEN & UNWIN
Sydney London Boston

© Bob Nicholls 1986
This book is copyright under the Berne Convention.
No reproduction without permission.
All rights reserved.

First published in 1986
Allen & Unwin Australia Pty Limited
8 Napier Street, North Sydney, NSW 2060, Australia

Allen & Unwin New Zealand Ltd
60 Cambridge Terrace, Wellington, New Zealand

George Allen & Unwin (Publishers) Limited
Park Lane, Hemel Hempstead, Herts HP2 4TE, England

Allen & Unwin Inc.
Fifty Cross Street, Winchester, Mass 01890, USA

National Library of Australia
Cataloguing in Publication entry:

Nicholls, Bob.
Bluejackets and Boxers.
Bibliography.
Includes index.
ISBN 0 86861 799 7.
1. Great Britain. Navy — Colonial forces — Australia.
2. China — History — Boxer Rebellion, 1899—1901.
3. Australia — History, Naval. I. Title.
951'.03

Library of Congress Catalog Card Number: 85-061874

Typeset in Goudy by Setrite Typesetters, Hong Kong
Printed by Koon Wah Printing Pte Ltd, Singapore

Front and back endpapers: G F Gregory
Detail from *HMCS Protector and the ship* Torrens 1885
watercolour and gouache with pencil 36.9 a 54.6 cm
Australian War Memorial (19821)

CONTENTS

Appendixes

MAPS

Maps by Cathy Wilcox

PREFACE AND ACKNOWLEDGEMENTS

B<small>LUEJACKETS</small> and Boxers is the first comprehensive study of Australia's long-forgotten initial military involvement in Asia. In 1900, five hundred sailors of the New South Wales and Victorian naval brigades and the South Australian warship *Protector* were sent to China as part of an international force raised to suppress the Boxer uprising.

The uprising was against foreigners, in particular missionaries, and their Chinese converts. Over 300 Westerners and 30 000 Chinese lost their lives. At the most dramatic stage of the uprising the Boxers laid siege to the foreign legations in Peking and a force of foreign troops was raised to rescue them.

I have deliberately adopted a popular rather than an academic approach to the topic, and I have made extensive use of the photographs available in Australia. The most important pictures come from the camera of Staunton Spain, who went to China with the New South Wales contingent as a lieutenant in the naval brigade. More than 100 of his glass-plate negatives survive, in collections in the Mitchell Library in Sydney and — renamed — in the Bracegirdle collection in the Australian War Memorial in Canberra. In the closing weeks of 1984 I spent some time in northern China 'walking the battle'. This gave me valuable general exposure into conditions in the area and an excellent framework within which to understand the accounts of several of the participants whose diaries survive. Unfortunately the diary of William Bertotto was not available at the time, so I was unable to retrace his fascinating steps, in particular those taken on the road to Pao-ting fu.

The inspiration for the book was my own but John Iremonger and Maggie Hamilton provided the initial encouragement. It would not have come to fruition without the assistance and encouragement of, in alphabetical order: Jim Atkinson, Tony Bennett, Gordon Clarke, R.J. Gill, Ross Gillett, Chris Hall, Lew Lind, R.H. Lofts, D.K. (Dusty) Miller, Christine Morrin, Peter Murnin, John Nicholls, Robyn Orr, and Jim Williams. The Command Photographic Centre, Naval Support Command, provided a high degree of technical expertise in working miracles with a number of unpromising-looking photographs, while at the War Memorial Ron Gilchrist and Steve Corvini pointed me in the right direction.

TABLES, MONEY AND CHINESE NAMES

METRIC CONVERSION TABLES

1 inch	= 25.4 mm	1 mile	= 1.61 km
1 foot	= 30.5 cm	1 nautical mile	= 1.852 km
1 yard	= 0.914 m	1 knot	= 1 nautical mile an hour
			= 1.85 km/h

CURRENCY

1 pound (£1) = $2.00
1 shilling (1s) = 10 cents
1 penny (1d) = 1.2 cents

COMPARABLE COSTS, 1900–1985

An Able Seaman's daily rate of pay of 7s or 7s 6d is quoted in the book. The 1900 rate of pay of a carpenter, plasterer, or semi-skilled worker, was about 9s 6d a day, and a labourer or navvy was paid 6s 10d.

A contemporary calculation of the daily expenses of a family of two adults and two children was:

3s	food
1s 4d	clothing
1s	rent
3s 4d	sundries (heating, medical, transport etc.)
8s 8d	*Total*

In 1900 bread cost 3d for a 2lb (1 kg) loaf
beef cost 3½d 1lb (500 g)
butter cost 11d 1lb (500 g)

In 1984 the average daily wage was $55.00 (550s); an Able Seaman in the Royal Australian Navy was paid $51.33 (513s) a day.

The correct rendering of Chinese names always presents a problem to an author. In this book I have chosen to use the spelling generally current at the time and have standardised individual variations in the sources. In the tables which follow, the old system was the name usually used by Westerners and pinyin is the Chinese equivalent. Pinyin is the phonetic alphabet system used by China to standardise the romanisation of Chinese names and places.

Old System	Pinyin
Dynasties	
Ch'ing	Qing
Ming	Ming
Tang	Dang
Natural features	
Gulf of Chihli	Bohai Wan
Hai Ho	Hai he
Pearl River	Zhu jiang
Pei Ho	Bei he
Yangtze Kiang	Chang jiang
Yellow River	Huang he
Yellow Sea	Huang hai
Provinces	
Chekiang	Zhejiang
Chihli	Zhili
Formosa (Taiwan)	Taiwan
Fukien	Fujian
Hopeh	Hebei
Kwangtung	Guangdong
Mongolia	Monggol
Shantung	Shandong
Tibet	Xizang

Cities and towns
(Some have changed their names completely.)

Canton	Guangzhou
Ching-huang-tao	Qinhuangdao
Kao-li-ying	Kuliushucun
Kiaochow	Qiaozhou
Mou-tou hsien	Moutou
Nanking	Nanjing
Pao-ting fu	Baoding
Peitang	Beitang
Peking	Beijing
Shan-hai-kwan	Shanhaiguan
Sin Ho (Shin Ho)	Xinhe
Taku	Daku
Tangku	Tanggu
Tientsin	Tianjin
Tsingtao	Qingdao
Tung-chao	Tongxian
Wei-hai-wei	Weihai
Woosung	Wusung
Yangtsen	Wuqing

INTRODUCTION

L
ATE in a winter's afternoon in 1900 an elderly man, dressed in the uniform of a naval captain and riding in an open carriage, took his position at the head of a procession which then left Fort Macquarie and set off up the slight rise into Macquarie Street. Behind the carriage came a bluejackets' band playing 'Sons of the Sea'. It was followed by 227 men in full naval marching order with swords and cutlasses at the 'ready' and fixed bayonets. At their head was Nipper, a brown and white eight-month-old bulldog pup with protruding teeth. Next came the entire New South Wales Marine Light Infantry, a corps less than a week old, while bringing up the rear was the balance of the New South Wales Naval Brigade and the Naval Artillery Volunteers. They were followed by a throng of civilians.

Passing through groups of cheering citizens lining their route, the procession made its way to Cowper Wharf at Woolloomooloo where, with little delay, the main body of 227 and Nipper marched on board the smartly painted steamship *Salamis* to join a similar-sized group of sailors who had recently arrived from Melbourne. Fifteen minutes later the troopship was moved by tugs a short distance to moorings in Farm Cove.

Earlier that morning the signal station at Cape Otway had reported the flagship of the South Australian Naval Force, HMCS *Protector*, heading east on a voyage from Adelaide to Sydney. Clearly some combined maritime enterprise was afoot.

This book is an account of that long-forgotten enterprise — the participation by the New South Wales, Victorian and South Australian colonial naval forces in the quelling of the Boxer uprising.

1

SETTING THE CHARGE

THE events in China which burst upon an incredulous outside world in June 1900 were a culmination of a centuries-long history of China's relations with other, principally Western, countries. There had been a trickle of trade with the Roman Empire, with Chinese silks being carried by land and sea to the Mediterranean in return for goods from central Asia and Greece. Later, Buddhism had been imported from India, then subsequently adapted to the essential Chinese philosophy, and in the Tang dynasty, around 650 A.D., Chinese armies were as far west as the shores of the Caspian Sea in central Asia.

By the time the Ming dynasty, founded by the Mongols, had assumed rulership of China in the middle of the fourteenth century, the eastern expansion of Europe in the Crusades, Italian commerce, and the missionary drives of the Franciscan and Dominican orders, had brought Europeans to the frontiers and shores of the Chinese empire. Relations between China and the West remained on a fairly amicable level until the overthrow of the Ming dynasty by the Manchus, who came sweeping into China from the north-east in 1644. By then, European maritime exploration, expansion and conquests of the sixteenth century had brought the Portuguese to India, Malacca, China and Japan and the Spaniards to the Philippines. By 1560 the Portuguese were established in Macao, an island off the southern coast of Kwangtung Province at the mouth of the Pearl River. From this small settlement they carried on trade with the Chinese.

Having taken over China by force, the Manchu conquerors established their own dynasty, the Ch'ing, and maintained permanent garrisons throughout the country. They ruled for the next three and a half centuries and, although they absorbed much of the Chinese culture and customs, they remained an essentially alien group who made sure that the risk of revolt was minimised by regularly moving their Chinese administrators from one part of the country to another.

Meanwhile, there was constant pressure from the yang kuei-tzu, the foreign barbarians or foreign devils, to enter China for religious and commercial reasons. On Macao, the Portuguese had been followed by the Dutch and the British; by the middle of the eighteenth century Britain was the most important foreign trader with China. However, except for Canton, European merchants had not been successful in their efforts to expand their trading activities to the Chinese mainland from the confines of Macao.

Chinese silks, cottons and tea were all the rage in Europe and were thus in great demand. For a time these goods were paid for in gold and silver, but as time went by the Chinese demand for opium meant that it took the place of currency. This demand became so great that the balance of trade was completely changed, with vast amounts of silver leaving the country to pay for the opium imported from India. Despite the fact that the importation of the drug had long been forbidden by the Manchu govern-

1

ment, corrupt Chinese officials connived at its introduction.

All trade with the West, which to all intents and purposes by now meant the British, was carried out through the port of Canton, where the Europeans had been allowed to settle a small enclave, called the 'factories'. In the 'off' season for trade they had to withdraw to Macao.

Although China, with an estimated population of about 350 million in 1800, was the largest country in the world, it was now in a slow decline. Viewing foreigners with increasing distaste, and set in its proud isolation, ancestor worship and suspicion of anything new, China eventually came to be at the mercy of those countries which had undergone an industrial revolution and which were becoming increasingly irritated with her exclusiveness. With the British merchants insisting on more privileges than the Chinese were disposed to concede, the stage was set for the initial conflict that resulted in anarchy and which led, a hundred years later, to the establishment of the Communist-ruled People's Republic of China.

In 1839, the central government in Peking finally took some vigorous action to stem the flood of opium flowing into the country through Canton. This high-handed attitude of interference with their legitimate trade didn't go down at all well with the British. Hostilities broke out and dragged on for three years, during which time the Chinese suffered repeated defeats. The war was concluded in 1842, with the signing of the Treaty of Nanking. Under the terms of the treaty the British were given the barren island of Hong Kong, an enormous sum of money as an indemnity, and permission to trade from ports other than Canton with the right to year-round residency.

This treaty was the turning point for China in her relations with the West. Taking advantage of the opportunity, other countries, led by the French, secured similar concessions from the beleaguered Chinese. Now that the floodgates were open, what amounted to an open season on China ensued for the remaining years of the nineteenth century and that once proud country underwent a humiliating series of pruning operations during which she was forced to relinquish vast tracts of land including Burma, the area which became French Indo-China, and many thousands of square miles in the northeast and north-west.

Taking a leaf from the westerner's books, the newly emerged Japan, which had converted itself from feudalism into a modern, western-style state, challenged China for possession of the ancient kingdom of Korea, and war broke out between the two countries in July 1894. The outcome was a foregone conclusion, with the unmodernised China being soundly defeated on land and at sea. At the treaty of Shimonoseki, signed in 1895, China renounced her claims to Korea, yielded Formosa (Taiwan), and had to part with another vast sum of money in reparations.

China's defeat at the hands of the Japanese confirmed to the rest of the world that the Ch'ing dynasty was on its last legs. As a consequence the major European powers hastily scrambled over the spoils of the helpless country, seeking 'spheres of influence' which, falling short of actual occupation in the manner of true colonists, meant that any country having a particular area of China as its 'sphere' would, de facto, run its affairs. At the beginning of 1900 this division of China into spheres of influence had roughly apportioned the country as follows:

Russia claimed Mongolia and Manchuria, and had also moved into the area around Peking.

Germany was pre-eminent in a band of country south of the Russian sphere which stretched from the Yellow Sea to Tibet and encompassed the Yellow River valley.

Britain claimed the whole of the Yangtze valley and the provinces to the south as well as most of Kwangtung.

Italy claimed Chekiang province.

Japan was active on the mainland in Fukien province opposite 'her' island of Formosa.

France claimed as her sphere of influence the provinces on China's southern borders where they abutted onto Indo-China.

This brief account of dismemberment shows that China's central government was on the

In 1860 the forts at Taku were stormed by a combined force of French and British sailors and marines prior to their march on Peking and the sacking of the Chinese capital. This well-known photograph shows the inside of one of the forts after it had been captured.

point of collapse at the hands of foreigners intent on dividing and occupying the country.

However, the northern Chinese peasants, from whose ranks the Boxers would come, knew nothing of the background to these events. It was the impact on them and their daily lives of two aspects of Western civilisation that brought about the uprising. These two facets were missionaries and railways.

The West's religious intrusion into China, which had been taking place for several centuries in one form or another, usually at low-level, intensified in the latter half of the nineteenth century.

In 1860, following an Anglo-French war with China during which the Taku Forts had been captured, Peking invaded and the Summer Palaces razed, the French had secured, by treaty, what amounted to a charter for all missionaries. Although it was originally intended to apply only to Roman Catholics, its provisions were subsequently extended to all denominations of the Christian faith. Under this treaty, missionaries were allowed residence anywhere in China, were protected by the Chinese authorities and their religion was officially recognised by the government.

The missionaries' formal association with the ruling classes did not endear them to the peasants, who were suffering the usual oppression from their official masters and were also having to put up with even higher than normal levels of corruption. Further friction was created by the missionaries' land demands for houses,

3

'A European Missionary In China Travelling as the Chinese do.' Missionaries' activities were largely responsible for the advent of the Boxers.

chapels and churches, whose tall spires created a disturbing impression and upset the feng shui — the art of siting structures in such a way as to maintain the delicate balance necessary to placate the twin spirits of wind and water.

Of course missionaries didn't restrict their activities to spreading the faith. The opening of orphanages to care for mainly female Chinese children who otherwise might have run the risk of being abandoned at birth or sold, led to the widespread suspicion that their young bodies were being required for some nefarious purpose. This fertile ground for arousing the superstitions of the peasant was paralleled by the activities of another group — the many medical missionaries. Although their secular professional work must have been blessed by many of their patients it was, for obvious reasons, scorned by local doctors and herbalists.

Equally ominous in the peasants' minds were the railways. Although at the end of the century there were only three comparatively short railway lines operating in China, many more were being surveyed or were under construction as a direct consequence of the scramble to exploit each international sphere of influence. As far as the Chinese were concerned, trains

The threat posed by the construction of railway lines also contributed to the rise of the Boxer movement. Normally, the (jin)rickshaw — a transliteration of the Chinese words for man-powered vehicle — and sedan chair were the main forms of transport for people in towns and carts pulled by ponies in the country.

were frightening, fire-eating dragons and obviously the work of devils. Furthermore, and here again feng shui became important, the tracks on which they were laid frequently violated a family's ancestral grave or other sacred site. Many peasants were convinced that it was a well-established practice of the barbarians to bury Chinese babies in the foundations of important structures such as cathedrals. The imminent construction of the permanent way would obviously require many more of these sacrifices to be made.

Something had to be done about the foreign devils. As the government seemed unwilling and unable to handle matters, it was a propitious time for the formation of a secret society.

2

LIGHTING THE FUSE

Protect the Ch'ing Dynasty,
Exterminate the Foreigner

. . . Boxer slogan

THE account in the preceding chapter of the situation in China to the turn of the twentieth century was based on generally accepted facts and their interpretation with the benefit of many years of *post facto* scholarly research into the subject. Such hindsight is of no benefit when describing the genesis of the Boxers, whose origins remain as obscure today as they were when they first came to the world's attention in 1898.

Secret societies have always played an important part in Chinese daily life. From all accounts this importance and influence on the Chinese mainland has been sharply curtailed in the years since the foundation of the People's Republic, but they are still strong in countries where many Chinese live such as Malaysia, Singapore and, to a less certain extent, Australia.

None has become quite as well known as the I He Tuan, the Righteous Harmony Group or Band. When they were first achieving their notoriety in northern China their name was somehow corrupted to I He Chuan which translated into Righteous Harmony Fists. From this it was a short step for the missionary free-lance correspondents for the Shanghai English-language newspaper the *North China Daily News* to coin the phrase the Boxers, and Boxers they have remained to the West to this day. Though there may be some doubt as to the correct name of this particular secret society, there is no doubt at all about its aim — to get rid of the foreigners in China by killing them all.

The general consensus is that the Boxers originated in the Shantung/Chihli border areas, to the south and east of Peking, and emerged as a direct consequence of German depredations in the areas as they stretched out their tentacles of trade emanating from Kiaochow/Tsingtao, which they had seized in 1897 as a reprisal for the murder of two German missionaries. By this time, however, the whole of north China had been for many years in a state of anarchy advanced even for that country and under that dynasty. Crops had failed, and there had been devastating floods. Relief measures, in the hands of the authorities in Peking, had proved next to useless. And matters had not been helped by a plague of locusts.

The Boxers' two targets were the foreigners, particularly the missionaries, and their Christian converts. Historians have been unable to unearth any evidence that they sought any advantages for themselves, either individually or as a group. Contemporary accounts cannot convincingly detect any leader in their ranks but there were certain movement-wide practices.

A Boxer's battle cry was a simple, uncom-plicated, even catchy, 'Sha! Sha!' ('Kill! Kill!'). His other activities, including complicated, prolonged and often hideous tortures, appear to have come naturally to the peasant who was the average adherent to the cause. The dress of a Boxer often consisted merely of a red shirt; but more important was his invulnerability to the foreigners' weapons. Demonstrations of this invaluable asset were frequent, with sword

Miss Mary L. Partridge was an American missionary at Taigu in Shanxi Province from 1893 until her death at the hands of the Boxers in 1900. She was one of 250 European missionaries or their families who lost their lives in the uprising. This 1890s photograph shows Miss Partridge and her Chinese helper about to start on an 'evangelistic tour of villages'.

slashes and pike-thrusts apparently having no effect on the dedicated practitioner. As Peter Fleming points out in his book *The Siege at Peking*:

> Accidents were, inevitably, caused by failures in the chicanery and legerdemain without which these tests must have proved either unconvincing to the audience or fatal to the actors; one keen fellow had the ill luck to be blown in two by a cannon-ball. But these miscarriages were glossed over by explaining that their victims had been lax in performing their devotions or had transgressed one of the numerous bye-laws of the Society.

Invulnerability is a particularly valuable asset for fighting a foe armed with modern weapons.

The Boxers' campaign first started to manifest itself in late 1898 and by early 1899 had taken the form of frequent attacks on the 'secondary devils' — the Chinese converted to Christianity. These attacks led to incidents of arson and finally murder, the latter often preceded by torture.

As the attacks increased in intensity, the question of their suppression by the Provincial and Peking authorities arose. In the province of Shantung suppression was in the nominal hands of the Governor, Yu Hsien, who, if not an ardent Boxer supporter, at least did not over-exert himself in putting the movement down and, as a result, the movement gathered momentum. Even in early 1900 when the Governor was replaced by a strong and able man, Yuan Shih-k'ai, edicts (proclamations from the throne) from Peking warned him to be 'extremely careful' in his dealings with the Boxers and he acted accordingly. Much the same occurred in neighbouring Chihli province, where the Governor was even weaker than his counterpart in Shantung. The situation was well on the way to getting completely out of hand when in January 1900, the Empress Dowager Tz'u-hsi, issued another edict that, reading between the lines as all Chinese had to do with such ambiguous pronouncements, gave full rein to the Boxers.

It was now only a matter of time before the general anti-foreign conflagration swept throughout northern China. By March 1900 the situation had become sufficiently serious for Britain, the United States and Italy to send warships to anchor off the north China port of Taku, at the mouth of the Hai Ho (River) in the Gulf of Chihli and the nearest ships of any size could get to the capital, Peking. This demonstration of naval power must have had little visual effect on those living on the coast and none at all on those, Boxers included, living inland since the ships were forced by the shallow waters of the Gulf of Chihli to anchor many miles offshore.

Coincidentally, things then seemed to quieten down, and precautions were relaxed, but by early May events worsened and reports began to reach the various legations in Peking of widespread arson and attacks on Christians throughout the whole of northern China. More to the point, there were reports of an imminent attack on the churches and legations in Peking itself.

By 28 May the situation in the countryside surrounding Peking was sufficiently bad for the Diplomatic Corps to request contingents of guards from their warships, which had returned to the waters off Taku and which had been reinforced by units from other countries. On 31 May detachments of bluejackets and marines, comprised of men from the United States, Britain, France, Italy, Japan and Russia, arrived in Peking by train from Tangku, the village on the railway line on the north bank of the Hai Ho opposite Taku, having been landed earlier in the day from their parent warships in

the Gulf of Chihli. This contingent, of 337 officers and men, was joined on 3 June by 52 German and 37 Austrian sailors.

Their arrival appeared to reduce tension in the capital itself, but more alarming reports of the murder of missionaries and civilians and widespread destruction of foreigners' property in the countryside around Peking forced the Diplomatic Corps to ask their admirals to dispatch further detachments. This request was made on 9 June. Next day the Commander-in-Chief of the China Station, Admiral Sir Edward Seymour, Royal Navy, the senior naval officer present, informed the Admiralty in London that in response to an urgent appeal from the British Minister in Peking he was landing at once with all available men. The force landed and, under Seymour's command, set off from Tientsin on the journey of two or three hours by train. It comprised just over 2000 bluejackets and

Commander-in-Chief of the Royal Navy's China Station, Admiral Sir Edward Seymour, landed in north China in June 1900 in command of a force of 2000 sailors and marines from several nations and set out to reinforce the legations in Peking. He was forced back by the Boxers and the Chinese Army.

marines, 900 of whom were British. The Germans had contributed 500 men and the Russians 300, with the balance made up of contingents from American, French, Italian, Japanese and Austrian warships. They were equipped with seven field guns and several machine guns.

Baggage carts were sent from the Peking legations to the railway terminus at Majiapu, just outside the southern city wall, to meet the contingents. Eventually they returned empty. Something had obviously gone seriously wrong.

To those who had stayed behind on their ships all seemed for a while to be going well, even though the telegraph line to Peking was cut, three days after the relief force had set out, severing communication with the legations. By 21 June, however, Rear-Admiral J.A.T. Bruce, Seymour's second-in-command, who had been left behind to take charge of the British fleet, was uneasy enough to signal to the Admiralty in London: 'No communication with Commander-in-Chief for seven days or Tientsin for five days.'

The worst fears of the pessimists in the legations had been realised — the Chinese Army had thrown in its lot with the Boxers. In a series of attacks on Seymour's force they had first halted it, at Anping, then forced it to beat a retreat in some disarray to the temporary, and by no means assured, security of a large Chinese arsenal they had stumbled across to the north of Tientsin, which itself was under siege.

Later that day, when the first information had been received about the fate of Seymour's force and the situation in and around Tientsin and when the magnitude of the disaster dawned on him, Bruce sent another signal reporting that casualties had been heavy, reinforcements were 'most urgently required', and that supplies of ammunition were insufficient. Pro tem a further small relief force was landed from the ships at Taku.

The situation in the legations in the capital was clarified a little later with a message from Peking from the Inspector-General of the Imperial Maritime Customs, Sir Robert Hart, in Peking. The message, delivered by hand in conditions of utmost peril by a young Englishman in the best 'Boy's Own' tradition, ran: 'Foreign community besieged in the legations. Situation desperate. Make haste.' The purport of the message was quite clear to Bruce. What he lacked, however, was the means to do anything to alleviate the situation, for he now had no forces left to land.

Royal Naval bluejackets advancing along the railway line north of Tientsin were halted and driven back near Anping by a combined force of Boxers and the Chinese Army.

Seymour's bluejackets and marines were forced to retreat along the Pei Ho to an arsenal outside Tientsin. They carried their wounded in junks hauled by their prisoners.

3

AUSTRALIA'S NAVIES

Every Hair a Spunyarn,
Every Finger a Marlinspike.

. . . description of sailor,
nineteenth century

URING the latter part of 1899 and 1900, there had been increasing mention in the world's press of the deteriorating situation in China. The Australian press was, however, in general occupied with more weighty topics such as Federation which, after many years of haggling and political to-ing and fro-ing was now looking a sure bet. In March 1900 delegates from the Colonies had gathered in London for the final pre-Federation session, and the Constitution Bill was to go before the British Parliament in July. Close attention was also being paid to the war in South Africa with the British motherland and the Boers where some 2500 regular troops and 3500 Citizen's Bushmen had been dispatched from all Australian Colonies. The exploits — and casualties — of the force were occupying a prominent place in the foreign news pages of the newspapers.

As 1900 wore on, a growing unease that all was not well in far-off Cathay was becoming apparent and by June the daily more alarming news had displaced most other foreign reports in the world's press.

Reports and headlines were one thing; dealing with the situation was an altogether different matter. Britain, with the bulk of her home army occupied in South Africa, was in a particularly difficult situation. It is therefore not surprising that, in addition to dispatching contingents from her Indian army to form the bulk of her land force response, she turned to other sources of military muscle to reinforce her maritime strength in the Far East. Some of this augmenting force, it was soon be be apparent, was to come from Australia. In the Australian colonial capitals too it was fast becoming clear that, if Britain was going to ask for help, their response would consist of bluejackets.

There were several reasons for the choice of sailors. First, the force that had gone to South Africa at the invitation of the British government the previous October and which had been added to constantly was comprised entirely of soldiers — both volunteers and regulars. By mid-1900 it was becoming increasingly difficult to recruit and train more soldiers to reinforce and replace contingents already dispatched. In these circumstances the diversion of military manpower to another, perhaps initially more popular, venture would be unwise. Next, traditionally, British martial adventures off in northern Cathay had always had a distinct nautical flavour to them, with episodes such as brushes with pirates, Yangtze River gunboats, and the storming of the Taku Forts in 1860. Finally, the men from the various naval brigades, which will be described shortly, had volunteered for the Australian Sudan force as far back as 1885 and, more recently, for the current war in South Africa. Their services had been spurned on each occasion.

But who were these sailors, where did they come from and what was their history?

The history of naval forces in Australian

The approaches to the fort at Taku stormed by the British and French in 1860. The scene inside the breach in the wall is shown in the illustration on page 3. The sharpened 'pungi' stakes will be familiar to Australians with experience in Vietnam. The forts were built almost entirely of mud.

waters dates, to all intents and purposes, from the period immediately prior to the outbreak of the Crimean War in 1854. The worsening of relations between Great Britain and Russia led to the first of the 'Threat From the North' or 'The Russians are Coming, the Russians are Coming' scares to which the colonies were to be treated on numerous subsequent occasions. The threat was apparently from the ships of the Russian fleet based at north Pacific ports. Exactly what form these assaults would take — raids on the colonies, invasion, attacks on shipping — was never made clear.

Naturally, the Royal Navy was responsible for the maritime defence of all British colonies, the Australian ones included. But in 1850 the Royal Navy's antipodean naval forces, based in Port Jackson, comprised only the 26-gun frigate HMS *Calliope*, a survey ship and four other small, elderly craft.

The need to respond to possible future Russian threats and, following the Gold Rush, to protect ships carrying the precious metal to

England led, in 1859, to the formation of the Australian Squadron of the Royal Navy. Its duties were to protect the colonies and the waters around Australia and New Zealand. In the meantime though, the impatient Victorian colonists had established their own navy, starting their fleet with Her Majesty's Colonial Ship (HMCS) *Victoria*, a steam sloop built in England in 1855−56 at a cost of £38 000. At 580 tons she was slightly larger than a present-day Sydney harbour ferry of the *Lady Street* class. *Victoria* remained the sole — and strictly speaking, illegitimate — full-sized Australian colonial warship until 1865.

The departure, in the late 1860s, of the last of the British army garrisons which had been in the colonies since their founding, coupled with the obvious lack of concern that the Admiralty was showing about the effectiveness of the Australian Squadron, led to the forming of a powerful local body of opinion which was concerned with the defence of the Australian continent. One consequence of the pressure they brought to bear on Whitehall was the passage, in Westminster, of the *Imperial Colonial Naval Defence Act*. Under the provisions of this Act, passed in 1865, individual colonies were empowered to raise naval forces for their coastal defence, thus making an 'honest woman' out of HMCS *Victoria* at long last. The intention was that the Royal Navy would still carry out what would nowadays be called the 'blue water' defence role for Australia.

The colonies may have been given the go-ahead to raise their own navies, but their efforts to translate that authority into practice were, in general, not impressive. The main problem was, as always, money. Whilst the colonies were quick to criticise the British for not providing an adequate naval umbrella, they were even more reluctant to contribute any money either to the Imperial coffers for the naval protection of the Empire as a whole or to their own colonial navies. Sometimes, it is true, they made spasmodic efforts to add to the puny strength of their naval forces, usually when there was a Russian scare, but in general the colonies were motivated entirely by self-interest.

The lithograph shows the Victorian Navy in 1886. The monitor Cerberus *is on the left of the illustration, with the gunboat* Albert *astern of her. In the right foreground is the torpedo boat* Childers *with the gunboat* Victoria *(the second ship to bear that name in the Victorian Navy) behind her. The elderly wooden line-of-battle ship* Nelson, *a sailing ship laid down in 1809 and converted to auxiliary steam propulsion later, is at the rear of the picture.*

Things came to a head in the mid-1880s when the British sent Admiral Tryon to take command of the Australia Station with instructions to talk the locals out of putting money, however little, into their own navies and instead to contribute more towards the presence of Imperial, i.e. Royal Navy, ships in Australian waters. Part of his brief was also to bring about the incorporation of these tiny local navies into the RN.

These proposals were not, to put it mildly, at all welcome to the Australian Premiers mainly because of the emerging Australian view that Australia should only be responsible for contributing to her own local defence.

An attempt to patch things up emerged from the 1887 Colonial Conference in London in the form of the *Australasian Defence Act* of the same year, which authorised the establishment of an Auxiliary Squadron in addition to the Royal Navy's Australian Squadron.

The Auxiliary Squadron was formed specifically to protect floating trade in Australasian, i.e Australian and New Zealand, waters. Although the ships were provided, manned and commanded by the Admiralty, they were in part to be paid for by the Australian colonies and New Zealand.

In return for their contribution, which comprised 5 per cent of the cost of constructing the squadron's ships and an annual maintenance

One of two almost-identical gunboats owned by the Queensland Marine Defence Force, HMQS *Gayundah*, with a displacement of 360 tons. The ship was built in 1883. In 1958 her hulk was beached at Redcliffe, on Moreton Bay, to provide a stable base for the cliff. Much of her 102-year-old steel hull is still there.

subsidy of £91 000, amounting in all to £126 000, Australians and New Zealanders were to be protected by a squadron of five third-class cruisers and two torpedo gunboats. What was novel in these arrangements was the stipulation of the Australian colonies, to which the British eventually agreed, that these warships could not be moved away from the Australia Station without the approval of the colonial governments. The arrival of the squadron in 1891 more or less brought the development of colonial navies to a halt.

Up until then New South Wales, Victoria, Queensland and South Australia had been the only colonies to raise and maintain naval forces under the 1865 Act. Tasmania possessed a torpedo boat with a displacement of 12 tons (about the weight of a single-deck bus and about as useful from a naval defence point of view), but it was manned, on the rare occasions it moved, by members of the colony's army.

By the turn of the century the Victorian Navy had long since disposed of its original flagship HMCS *Victoria* and had replaced her with the by now 30-year-old monitor, Her Majesty's Victorian Ship (HMVS) *Cerberus*, which had been constructed in England in 1870 with a grant of £100 000 from the British government. (There was a lack of uniformity and consistency to the honorifics preceding a ship's name in the Australian colonial navies. Queensland and Victoria had incorporated their colony's name, while South Australia and New South Wales, perhaps because of the number of words in their state name, preferred 'Colonial'). The remainder of the force consisted of five small torpedo boats.

By the mid-1880s Queensland had formed a navy and ordered two gunboats but, as a consequence of financial restrictions which plagued the colony, HMQ ships *Gayundah* and *Paluma* spent much of their pre-Federation careers as either a survey ship on loan to the Royal Navy (*Paluma*) or laid up (*Gayundah*). By the end of the century neither ship could be described as being in good condition.

HMCS *Protector*, described by the press as a gunboat, had been ordered by the South Australian government from the British firm of Sir Wm Armstrong & Co. of Newcastle-upon-Tyne in 1882 and had been delivered to Adelaide on 30 September 1884. She was, more

A mid-Victorian wood engraving of the South Australian gunboat Protector *gives an impression of the ship, classed as a cruiser, which probably shows her appearance on arrival in South Australia from the United Kingdom in the mid-1880s.*

correctly, a very small steel-hulled cruiser with an overall length of 185 feet and a beam of 30 feet. Her draught was 12 feet 6 inches, and her displacement was 920 tons. She was much smaller than the present-day RAN survey ship HMAS *Cook*.

For her size she carried a very heavy armament of one 8-inch, five 6-inch and four 3-pounder guns as well as Gatling guns. Two engines, each of 750 horsepower, gave the ship a design speed of fourteen knots, but in practice this had been reduced to about ten or eleven knots due to age. A more complete description of the *Protector* appears in Appendix V and further technical details of her armament in Appendix VI. The ship had been comparatively well maintained in spite of the colony's periodic severe financial difficulties, even though she had often been employed on non-military duties.

Last, and in this case, least, of the colonial navies were the New South Wales naval forces. For a number of reasons, partly financial but also partly due to the presence in Port Jackson of 'mummy's apron strings' in the form of the Royal Navy's Australian Squadron and, later, the Auxiliary Squadron behind which the Mother Colony could take cover, New South

Wales had what can only be described as a dismal record as a would-be naval power. By the end of the century the fleet consisted of two 22-ton outrigger torpedo boats, HMCS *Acheron* and HMCS *Avernus*, built in the Sydney suburb

One of the four Hotchkiss breech-loading 3-pounder quick-firing guns on HMCS Protector. *The gun, which was designed to ward off attacks by small, fast torpedo boats, fired a 3-pound shell to a range of about 3400 yards. The gun required a normal crew of 3. The ammunition was fixed i.e. the shell and cartridge were supplied in one piece, with the propellant charge contained in the same way as a rifle bullet, in a brass cartridge case.*

Sham fight, Fort Denison, Sydney Cove 1881. The photograph illustrates an early example of a 'Shop Window' exercise, when a navy shows off its might to the public. The presence of such a comparatively powerful squadron of the Royal Navy in Sydney meant that New South Wales saw little need for spending money on their own naval forces. Note the crowds of spectators afloat for the occasion, including far too many on board what has become a somewhat unstable ferry.

of Pyrmont in the late 1870s at a cost of £4000 each. They had been designed to be used inside the harbour of Port Jackson and were kept out of the water for much of their lives.

So much for the ships in the five colonial navies' order-of-battle. What of the men?

Generally speaking, each colony with warships kept them running by utilising a small core of full-time professional seamen and engineers, augmenting them at training times with reservists. These reservists, the majority of whom tended to be volunteers drawn from the ranks of retired, mainly Royal Navy, seamen, were formed into naval brigades. The concept of a naval brigade seemed to embrace providing the balance — a majority — of the crews for the ships of their own colony's navy in time of crisis, defending the coastline, and acting as landing forces should they be so required.

As an example, the New South Wales naval brigade was formed in 1863 as a consequence of an announcement which appeared in the *Sydney Morning Herald*.

A proclamation has been issued by command of His Excellency the Governor authorising the formation of a Volunteer Naval Brigade and prescribing the following terms and conditions upon which the offers of services in the said Naval Brigade will be accepted on behalf of Her Majesty.

1   Volunteers will be enlisted under the powers conferred by the Act 18 Victoria No. 8;

2   Commissioned officers will be appointed by the Governor;

3   Clothing, arms, accoutrements and ammunition will be issued by the Government under Regulations which will be hereafter notified;

4   The Naval Brigade is to consist of three companies of forty men each in Sydney.

This historic and damaged photograph of the officers was probably taken soon after the New South Wales Naval Brigade was formed in 1863.

Captain Francis Hixson, Royal Navy, was soon to be appointed, at a rate of pay of five shillings a day, to be in command of the brigade and was still in command 37 years — and several pay

Mrs Macquarie's Fort, Sydney, March 1871. Fort Macquarie, on Bennelong Point, was the headquarters of the New South Wales Naval Brigade for the last half of the nineteenth century. The fort was demolished in 1901 and a tram station was built there. The site is currently occupied by an opera house.

rises — later. Brigade headquarters and drill hall were at Fort Macquarie, on Bennelong Point. The Fort became a tram depot in 1901 and the site is now occupied by an opera house. At the height of one of 'The Russians are coming, the Russians are coming' scares the brigade was reported to be capable of fielding over 600 men, but by the end of the nineteenth century the average strength had dwindled to little over 300 men.

By 1886 the Naval Artillery Volunteer Company (NAV) had been raised and added to Captain Hixson's command. This unit had been formed to man the flagship, the wooden-hulled screw corvette HMCS *Wolverene*, in addition to their coast defence artillery tasks, but had seen little service as the ship had rarely stirred from her moorings in Farm Cove and had been disposed of in 1891.

Whilst the numbers borne on the books of the naval brigade were kept at a respectable level during Captain Hixson's 37 years of command, the general level of training and state of equipment suffered a gentle but distinct decline. As already noted there had been no

The wooden-hulled screw corvette Wolverene *was built for the Royal Navy in the early 1860s and in 1882 was given to the colony of New South Wales as a 'royal gift' when the Royal Navy no longer had any use for her. She was employed as a training ship for the New South Wales naval forces but rarely went to sea. The ship was sold in 1892.*

sea-going training for the force since the early part of the decade, when the *Wolverene* had made her final voyage to Jervis Bay. In the absence of sea training it might have been thought that the brigade would have concentrated on coast defence, their secondary role. The degree to which this aspect of training had been followed was evinced by a newspaper report in early July 1900 when an officer of the brigade, then, as is often the case nowadays, preferring to remain anonymous, was quoted as saying: 'We can't equip a single man. We have not even a water-bottle, nor have we any haversacks for the men. As regards our arms, the machine guns are obsolete; we have only the old pattern Martini-Henry rifles, and in fact no field kit of any description could be taken to the front.' Or, in the words of another account: '. . . the Brigade having no outfit or gear, could not even hold an encampment for a few days on the shores of Port Jackson.' According to other reports the brigade had not even undertaken its sole annual training commitment, an Easter camp, for six years.

Still, a country cannot expect too much in the way of navy when it spends £8000 a year on the service, as in New South Wales in 1897. Particularly when its commanding officer was paid £500 of that sum and the majority of the balance was disbursed as wages to the men for their periodic attendances at drill nights. However, each man had a uniform, boots and gaiters and sufficient other basic equipment to go on parade and the brigade's band was fully manned with competent musicians and had a high professional reputation. To the casual civilian observer then the naval brigade was a viable defence force for the colony. What is more the *Sydney Morning Herald* had said so:

> . . . as regards its drill and stamina of its members, each successive Admiral [of the Australasian Squadron] has highly praised the Naval Brigade, and their appearances at the Queen's Birthday review and other functions is always the signal for public approbation.

According to a contemporary report, of the 328 men on the books of the brigade, 78 per

The stretcher party of the New South Wales Naval Brigade on the occasion of Queen Victoria's Diamond Jubilee on 22 June 1897. Their summer hats are made of sennit, a type of plaited and woven cord. The men are wearing leather equipment and bayonets indicating that in those days they had a combatant role as well as one of caring for the wounded. This did not change until the Geneva Convention came into general international usage in 1910.

cent had joined on leaving the Royal Navy, having presumably taken their discharge from ships either on the Australia Station or the East Indies or China Stations then working their way to Australia to become settlers. A further 16 per cent were said to be Royal Navy Reserve men, indicating that at one time they had served in the Royal Navy, and the balance, with the exception of four men who were allegedly 'crack rifle shots', were former merchant seamen. There was obviously no doubt at all about the competence of these men as seamen — the phrase 'every hair a spunyarn, every finger a marlinspike' might have been coined especially for them.

In 1900 the brigade was still under the command of Captain Francis Hixson. He first came to the colonies in 1848 as a junior officer in HMS *Savannah*. Later, he had been appointed as navigating lieutenant of HMS *Herald*, then employed on survey duty on the Australian coasts, and had served on board that ship for

nine consecutive years. He had retired from the Royal Navy in 1863, perhaps seeking a change, to take up the appointment of Superintendent of Pilots and Lighthouses for New South Wales. Of his standing in the community there was no doubt, but as to his fitness to take command of any contingent, serious questions as to his age, coupled with his complete lack of experience in modern naval warfare, both at sea and on land, must have arisen.

Across the border in Victoria things were a lot more impressive. This was due in the main to the presence of the *Cerberus*, which had a permanent crew of 90 officers and men, as well as 45 permanent staff at naval depots at Port Melbourne and Williamstown. The colony's naval reserve force numbered 150. The five torpedo gunboats, when combined with a small force of auxiliaries, provided some opportunity for reserve officers and sailors alike to keep their nautical hands in.

The Victorian Navy was also fortunate in

Members of the New South Wales Naval Brigade at drill, with their 'Yataghan' rifle bayonets being used as swords. Gunnery Instructor Rickwood, on the left of the photograph, is in charge of the group, while a midshipman looks on. The photograph was probably taken in Sydney shortly before the Boxer uprising took place.

that it had had a succession of energetic officers in command, with Commander F.R. Tickell, who had taken over the force in 1897, firmly in control by mid-1900.

The Ironclad Monitor Cerberus *at practice in Hobson's Bay, 29 September 1871. The ship was 30 years old in 1900 and was quite unsuitable for service in China. The lithographer has used a certain amount of artistic licence in his portrayal of the ship.*

Queensland had naval brigades but little relevant material exists about their capabilities.

The one-ship navy that was the South Australian Naval Force had largely restricted itself to a reserve which, on mobilisation, formed the balance of the crew of the gunboat/cruiser *Protector*.

The ship was manned in normal times with a skeleton permanent staff of a few officers and key chief and petty officers. In mid-1900 the head of the service, Captain C.J.Clare, had only just taken over as Commandant of the Force, replacing a Captain William Rooke Creswell R.N. retired, who had moved to Queensland to become the Commandant of the Marine Defence Force there.

In so far as they were able, with their lack of finance, personnel and ships, to follow any naval doctrine, the colonial navies, for obvious reasons, took their ideas straight from the Royal Navy which, by the end of the nineteenth century, had completed the best part of eight decades as the world's unchallenged maritime watchdog.

The Victorian Naval Reserve. The wood engraving from the magazine The Australasian
Sketcher *of April 1882 gives an artist's impression of the uniform and equipment of the
officers and men of the Victorian Naval Reserve. If the illustration is anything to go by, some
of the men of the Reserve at least were not in their first flush of youth.*

HMCS Protector *Field Gun's Crew. 12 June 1897. A landing party sometimes needed to take their own artillery with them when they went ashore. Chief Gunner E. Argent, in the centre of the photograph, was the* Protector's *gunner and their instructor, and went to China with the ship. The type of gun cannot be seen in the photograph, but it is possible that it was a ten-barrelled Gatling gun.*

Many decades of acting in the role of international policeman had resulted in a wealth of experience in the use of sailors as soldiers for limited periods. The landing of armed parties of sailors, on some occasions several thousand strong, from ships of the Royal Navy, for repression of slavery on the West African coast, for bringing recalcitrant tribespeople to heel, perhaps with a whiff of grapeshot, for providing succour to earthquake or tidal wave victims, and for rounding up pirates or destroying their lairs were far more common occurrences to the crew of a man-of-war than gunnery practice or manoeuvring with other ships to practise battle tactics. A sizable naval brigade had been on active service in South Africa since the outbreak of hostilities there.

In these circumstances it is not surprising that the naval brigades of the colonies would claim to have some expertise in operations onshore, particularly when so many of their non-commissioned officers and ratings had been in the ranks of the Royal Navy and would therefore have had plenty of first-hand experience of this feature of nineteenth-century naval life.

It would be natural then for the British to consider naval forces first when dealing with the serious situation in northern China in late June 1900.

4

MAKE ME AN OFFER . . .

L ORD Brassey, the late Governor of Victoria, arrived at Southampton in England on 27 June after relinquishing his colonial post. Having been at sea for some weeks he was probably a little out of touch with the sentiments of the colonies, but nevertheless was able to state firmly that Australia would 'readily co-operate with the Imperial authorities in the Chinese War'. Coincidentally perhaps, the next day the Secretary of State for the Colonies, Mr Joseph Chamberlain, dispatched the following cable to the Governor of South Australia, who forwarded copies to his colleagues in the other colonies:

London 28 June

The Admiralty states that additional ships of light draught capable of navigating the Yangtze Kiang and other rivers are urgently required in China. No vessels of this class are ready here. It would take them six or seven weeks to get out to China when ready, while vessels from Australia could reach Hong Kong in three weeks.

Her Majesty's government would be glad therefore, if your responsible advisers would consent to the immediate despatch to China of three vessels from the Australasian Squadron, [He meant the Australian Squadron, but the names seem to have been interchangeable both in Whitehall and the colonial capitals alike] one of the Katoomba class, one of the Mohawk class, and one gunboat.

Three ships of the squadron, now in reserve, would be commissioned with crews to be sent out at once to replace these vessels on the Australian Station.

The matter is of great urgency, as applications for gunboats for the protection of life and property are pouring in from consuls, and assent from Australian colonies would be gratefully appreciated by Her Majesty's Government.

J. Chamberlain

Of the ships mentioned two, the third-class steel cruiser HMS *Mohawk* and the gunboat HMS *Lizard*, were part of the Royal Navy's Australian Squadron. The request for their release was therefore a matter of politeness. The third ship, the third-class cruiser HMS *Wallaroo*, was a unit of the Auxiliary Squadron and so under the provisions of the Australasian Defence Act of 1887 required formal colonial government approval before she could leave Australian waters. All ships mentioned were manned entirely by British bluejackets.

The reference in the Secretary of State's cable to the dispatch of additional crews from England to man replacement ships highlighted the fact that the Auxiliary Squadron had been allowed to run down to the state where 50 per cent of its strength was in reserve. Perhaps more significantly, it also might reflect the Admiralty opinion that the colonial naval forces lacked the necessary competence to man, let alone steam, them despite the understanding that the Act had made provision for their training in the ships of this squadron. It should also be noted

HMS Mohawk, *a third-class cruiser of 1770 tons, was one of the ships of the Royal Navy's Australian Squadron dispatched by the British government to China in July 1900.*

HMS Wallaroo, *a 2575-ton third-class cruiser of the Auxiliary Squadron, was one of five ships specifically allocated for the defence of Australia under the provisions of the Australasian Defence Act of 1887. She had a complement of 245 and an armament of eight 4.7-inch quick-firing guns and eight 3-pounder quick-firers. The colonial governments had to give their permission before ships of the squadron could be sent away from Australia.*

that nothing was said in Chamberlain's cable about any Australian colonial contribution to the Empire's cause.

The arrival of the request spurred the colonial governments into action. First off the mark was the government of Victoria, who replied almost immediately. The first of two cables sent back to the mother country on Friday 29 June came from the Lieutenant Governor, Sir John Madden, who had replaced Lord Brassey:

> To the Secretary of State for the Colonies
>
> Referring to your telegram of 28th June, my ministers cordially assent to Admiralty's proposals for despatch of men of war of Australasian squadron as requested, and they will take steps to give their help in the matter.

What these steps were became clearer after a meeting of the Victorian cabinet at noon that day when the Minister of Defence, Mr Melville, reported that he had been informed by Captain Tickell (Commander F.R.Tickell, the Commander of the Victorian Navy, was frequently referred to in dispatches and the press as Captain Tickell), that 200 well-trained naval men could be equipped and sent from Victoria to Hong Kong at less than a week's notice. So carried away were the normally cautious politicians by recognising a chance to steal a march on the other colonies, that they subsequently approved the following supplementary telegram for dispatch to Mr Chamberlain:

> By vessels of the Australasian squadron or by a special transport we can despatch to China, *at our own expense* [emphasis mine], within a week, 200 well-trained naval men and officers, with two 14-pound quick-firing guns on field carriages if desired. Reply.

Following hard on the heels of the Victorians, the Queensland government cabled London on 30 June that they 'had no objection whatever to the proposals'. The Premier went on to offer the use of the gunboats *Paluma* or *Gayundah* 'should either of them be desired for service in China

waters'. This offer was made on the understanding that the gunboat would be manned by British officers and bluejackets.

In Perth, Sir John Forrest, the Premier of Western Australia, confined his colony's commitment to concurring with the views of his eastern colleagues and sent telegrams to this effect to the Premier of New South Wales and Mr Chamberlain. This was the extent of the colony's involvement.

The South Australian government were next in line. On Monday 2 July they requested the Governor, Lord Tennyson, to reply to Mr Chamberlain's telegram, 'freely consenting'. Following a second Cabinet meeting that day, a further telegram was sent, this time offering the services of their pride and joy (and their fleet), the cruiser HMCS *Protector*.

The fine print in this offer and the consequential unedifying haggling that ensued will

Sir William Lyne was the Premier of New South Wales at the time of the dispatch of the men of the colony's naval brigade to China in 1900. The Victorians called his efforts to recruit a contingent 'a regrettable fiasco' and 'a bungle'.

be discussed in the next chapter.

The mother colony, New South Wales, went further. The Premier, Sir William Lyne, had received Chamberlain's telegram through the Governor, Lord Beauchamp, at the same time as the other Premiers. His reply not only concurred with the proposed dispatch of the warships from the Australasian Squadron but added a proposal for specific New South Wales assistance to the Imperial cause. This was the suggestion that the New South Wales naval forces themselves should man one or more of the ships of the Auxiliary Squadron which were in reserve and steam them to China to take part in operations there. The implication of this suggestion, which was reported in the Sydney *Daily Telegraph* on 4 July, was that the costs of the forces would be borne by the Imperial government.

HMS Tauranga, *a third-class cruiser of the Auxiliary Squadron, was in reserve in Sydney in 1900. The initial New South Wales offer was to provide the crews for one or more of the ships of the squadron which were in reserve and steam them to China to take part in operations there. The Admiralty rejected this idea.*

At first glance the proposal to man the ships with New South Welshmen sounded like a good idea. The third-class cruiser HMS *Tauranga* and the torpedo gun boat HMS *Karrakatta* were lying in reserve off Garden Island with only shipkeepers (watchmen) on board. The ships fitted the criteria laid down in Mr Chamberlain's cable asking for permission to release other ships of the squadron in that they were of a draught

shallow enough for navigating the Yangtze and other Chinese rivers. They were also simple ships to operate.

Replying to the New South Wales cable, Chamberlain stated how 'gratified' he was and that he had referred the offer to the Admiralty. While their Lordships were pondering this, the Premier and Mr See (the Minister of Defence for the colony) were able to fob off enquiries. The Premier explained to a reporter that the government had not resolved upon any definite course of action, that Ministers did not wish to act rashly, and that whether volunteers would be called on would depend on circumstances. 'If volunteers are wanted,' he went on, 'there will be any number of men coming forward.' His belief was probably based on an interview with Hixson, who had assured him of the willingness of his men to take part in any expeditionary force sent to quell the 'heathen Chinee'. Meanwhile, in an example of the flag following trade, the New South Wales Agriculture Department had been instructed by the Premier to cable the Agent-general (the colony's representative) in London that the colony could, if necessary, supply any quantity of foodstuffs and fodder for delivery to China. Having dealt with affairs of state — or at least of colony — Premier Lyne then took off for a week's tour through the New South Wales countryside.

The attitude of the Victorians was in marked contrast. Here the enthusiasm of both the naval forces and the government seemed to know no bounds, due to a great extent by the fortuitous fact that Commander Tickell had as the Secretary of the colony's Department of Defence a retired naval officer, Commander Collins. Added to this happy coincidence was the fact that, as previously noted, the colony actually had a trained navy in existence. Tickell's first suggestion was to re-acquire and re-commission the elderly gunboat *Albert* and dispatch it as the colony's contribution. Second thoughts on the practicability of this suggestion soon caused it to be abandoned. Both *Victoria* and her consort, *Albert*, had been placed out of commission some years previously and were now

One of the 14-pounder Maxim—Nordenfeldt quick-firing guns on HMCS Cerberus. Two of these guns were unshipped and fitted onto carriages made by the Victorian Railways for the Victorian contingent to take to China with them.

very much demilitarised. Thus the Victorian response, though enthusiastic, was perforce limited to one of men.

The enthusiasm was, in the political sense, due to a need to be 'one-up' on the rest of the Australian colonies. So keen was this competition, and so keen were the Victorian government to let the electorate and the other colonies know their plans, that they leaked the contents of Mr Chamberlain's cable, which had been classified 'Secret' — a high classification for those days. This early example of a breach of security for political purposes resulted in an annoyed cable from London and some sharp remarks from the other colonial governments. By the middle of the next week London, their Lordships having considered the Victorian offer, replied with another cable accepting the proposal.

As the way was now clear, enrolment of the men started on Saturday 7 July. That morning Commander Tickell had the permanent force paraded before him on board HMVS *Cerberus*. He explained the conditions of service and then called for volunteers. Seventy-seven men, four

officers and six gunners stepped forward; the majority of the crew that had mustered. Attendance at the parade at Port Melbourne was, due to short notice, somewhat lower than normal. Nevertheless, of those on parade 35 men and five officers stepped forward. Absent from this first batch of volunteers was Able Seaman William J. Bertotto. Fortunately for our understanding of the subsequent adventures of the brigade in China, he later volunteered and was accepted at the beginning of the next week. At Williamstown naval depot three petty officers and 26 men enrolled.

The problem of the men having been satisfactorily settled — or at least come within sight of settlement — the matter of equipment came next. Here again, Victoria was in a far happier position than her colleagues across the border to the north, and by 10 July the Melbourne *Age* was able to report 'excellent progress is being made in clothing and equipping the contingent. As far as accoutrements are concerned, everything was well within sight yesterday [9 July]. Each man will get his full kit in one issue.'

To produce a balanced force the Victorians

The Victorian contingent's 14-pounder guns after they had been mounted on the mountings made by the Victorian Railways. In the photograph sailors of the naval brigade are trying out their new acquisitions. It looks as if each limber had stowage for about sixteen shells and propellant charges. The outfits were exchanged for more modern weapons in Hong Kong.

also intended to take their own artillery in the form of two Maxim–Nordenfeldt 14-pounder quick-firing guns landed from HMVS *Cerberus*. Unfortunately the guns were not supplied with carriages and limbers for land use. The solution the resourceful Victorians adopted was to build their own, and the government's railway workshops at Newport were set to work designing and manufacturing them.

It will be remembered that the Victorian government, perhaps rashly, had offered to bear the cost of raising and dispatching their contribution. This was covered by the passage in the Victorian Parliament of an appropriation of £20 000 'to defray the expenses of the naval contingent for the East'. Naturally this money had to be accounted for, as did the supplementary funds required when the original appropriation was exhausted. Fortunately the account book survives in the archives of the Australian War Memorial. These accounts show that the cost of making the carriages and limbers for the 14-pounder guns was £500 10s 6d, with 12 wheels for the carriages, limbers and ammunition wagons costing £138, while the manufacture of the carriages and miscellaneous items amounted to £333 10s 6d. In the clothing department 378 flannel suits cost £179 9s 3d, 214 serge jumpers were £176 11s 0d, 213 (!) serge trousers were

£159 15s 0d and 400 pairs of sox [sic] cost the Victorian taxpayer £20 16s 8d.

Now that the contingent was respectably (although, as it transpired, not entirely appropriately) clothed the martial aspects of their expedition had to be accounted for:

79 000 cartridges, SA Ball .303
Martini–Enfield — £474 0s 0d.

12 000 cartridges, pistol Webley £45 0s 0d.

396 cartridges, pistol Enfield £1 5s 9d.

Four pairs of field glasses, engraved and stamped, were purchased for £24 0s 0d, and nineteen swords were sharpened at 2s 6d a blade.

By 11 July the contingent had been selected and medically examined by the doctor who was to accompany them to China, Staff Surgeon Stewart, the surgeon to the Victorian naval forces. They were kitted up with uniform, accoutrements and first field dressings (two, costing 10d each, for each man) and waiting for the call to be sworn in. The Victorian Premier was then able to ask London for details of the transport arrangements for the contingent, implying that, south of the border anyway, they were all set to go.

Meanwhile, there were going-away parties to attend. Typical of these affairs was one held at Fitzroy on Saturday 14 July:

> A pleasant gathering of the employees of Messrs John Sharp and Son took place on Saturday evening at Webber's Rose of Melbourne Hotel, to say farewell to two of their comrades, Messrs Fletcher and Raeymacker, who are members of the Naval Contingent for China. The social hall was nicely decorated for the occasion with Chinese [!] lanterns, streamers of red, white and blue were predominant, and the supper table was beautifully decorated with ferns and flowers. An interesting programme of songs, &c., was gone through. Mr Fletcher was presented with a handsome morocco dressing case and silver matchbox, suitably inscribed, and Mr Raeymacker with a silver matchbox.

Heaven knows what kind of action his workmates expected Able Seaman Fletcher to encounter for them to consider a 'handsome morocco dressing case' as a suitable parting present.

At a somewhat grander social occasion, at a 'send-off' given by the people of Williamstown to Commander Tickell and his men, he said, in part, that the whole contingent was proud to be bound on active service (Applause). He hoped they would have plenty of it, and that the commanding officer in China would do to them as David did to Uriah — put them in the thickest part of the fight (Applause). He hoped they would be worthy of fighting alongside their brethren in the Imperial service. They had all worked together and they had all been retrenched together (Loud laughter and applause). They were now going to fight together (Cheers).

Details of the force finally sworn in for service in China, whose names appear in Appendix III, reveal that the average age was about 35 with more than three-quarters of them married. This reflected the base from which the naval contingents were drawn, and was in contrast to the soldiers going to South Africa, whose average age was 22 or 23 and who tended to be single. The majority of volunteers worked in Port Melbourne or Williamstown. Their employers generally gave them leave of absence, thus guaranteeing them a job on return. One exception was Mr Edwards, a member of the Williamstown division of the naval brigade. Edwards, who had been employed by the Williamstown Gas Company as a stoker for twelve years, applied to the directors of the company for leave of absence. This was refused. He was informed that *if* he returned he would have the first chance when a vacancy occurred. In consequence he left his job with them. The account of this patriotic demonstration went on to mention that the duties of the stokers at the Williamstown Gas Company required them to work seven days a week, with two days' holiday a year.

In a cable dated 7 July Joseph Chamberlain dashed the hopes of the New South Wales brigade getting some sea-experience manning British ships. In his reply the Secretary of State for the Colonies said:

> ... Admiralty highly appreciate desire of officers and men of Naval Brigade to serve in China: as all ships are fully manned cannot be utilised for ordinary man-of-war duties, but if prepared to serve as Naval Brigade with expedition for protection of British life and property could render invaluable service. Telegraph on what terms as to payment if offer is made and whether brigade would take any guns, rifles and ammunition with them, and if so what quantity and description. Should at first proceed to Hong Kong.

This reply also put a stop to the alternative plan that had originated within the ranks of the brigade of supplying a make-up crew for HMS *Europa*, a Royal Navy cruiser which was about to sail from Sydney for Batavia. The brigade's plan was for their colonial contingent to make up what was understood to be a 300-man deficiency in her crew and for the then fully complemented ship to proceed to China. This rejection of the New South Wales offer may have been in part due to the Victorian offer which had been non-specific as to employment of their men and a desire by the Admiralty to arrive at some uniformity in the Australian contribution. There is also the suspicion that perhaps successive Royal Navy admirals, while publicly praising the naval brigades after their annual inspections for their bearing on the parade ground, had been making other appraisals of their military effectiveness in their reports to their superiors at the Admiralty.

After a couple of days absorbing this disappointing news the brigade and the NAV were assembled at their barracks at Fort Macquarie so that Captain Hixson could explain the conditions of service now proposed and register the names of those wishing to volunteer. Only those of robust health and aged between eighteen and 45 would be accepted and their term of service would be guaranteed until dispensed with by the naval authorities in China. The rate of pay would be 5s a day for ABs, 5s 6d for second-class petty officers and 6s for first-class petty officers. According to a report of the meeting:

> The force was then dismissed for a short time to give the men the opportunity of discussing the terms offered.
>
> On reassembling it was apparent that certain difficulties had arisen, as the response was poor. Amongst the NAV only 26 men and no officers handed in their names; whilst of the Naval Brigade three officers and not a single man stated their willingness to enlist.

There were several reasons given for this state of affairs, including the suggestion that the men were not willing to serve on land, having volunteered for sea service; that members of the brigade objected to sharing their status with the NAV and, as far the NAV were concerned, that they believed it was their duty to defend their own coasts. Finally, it was suggested very tentatively in some quarters that it just might be due to the fact they were being offered 5s a day while their counterparts in Victoria, on 7s 6d per day, would be drawing 50 per cent more.

The anomaly arose because of a difference between the Imperial i.e. Royal Navy/British Army rates of pay and those of the colonial military forces. The problem was not a new one

— it had emerged recently in the matter of pay for the contingents sent to South Africa, where the colonial governments had made up the difference between the 'Imperial' daily rate and the amount received by the soldiers from the colonies. At that time the basic pay for an able seaman in the Royal Navy was 1s 9d a day. What is difficult to comprehend is the pious hope of the New South Wales government that they could get away with such parsimony.

Their predicament did not go unnoticed south of the New South Wales border and by Monday 16 July the Melbourne newspapers were gleefully referring to the efforts to recruit the New South Wales contingent as a 'regrettable fiasco'. However their remarks were perhaps tempered a little by the realisation that if the New South Welshmen didn't get their act together soon the authorities in London might dispense with the services of the Australian colonial navies entirely, and the opportunity to take part in active service, with all its attendant excitements and glory, might be lost. This attitude was probably behind the inquiry from the Victorian Premier to his New South Wales counterpart on 17 July, which asked, 'What are you doing? Our contingent is ready to sail.' This elicited the lame reply from Sir William Lyne: 'I have been very busy today, hope to be able to give you an answer tomorrow.' There was no answer, 'tomorrow' or any other day.

Lyne was also under pressure from London, as a cable from the Colonial Office of 17 July makes clear:

> Admiralty have proposed that naval brigade shall be paid at imperial rates from imperial funds; difference between imperial and colonial rates to be paid by colony but necessary sanction not yet received. In the meantime detailed statement required as to composition of contingent in order that cost of payment at imperial rates may be estimated. Telegraph reply.

Two days later, on 19 July, matters were brought to a head by the announcement that the Admiralty had engaged a transport, the SS *Salamis*, to take the Victorian and New South Wales contingents to China. And all this against the backdrop of daily sensational reports from China, culminating in the news of the 16 July massacre of all the beleaguered Europeans in the capital. As the Melbourne *Age* put it smugly but succinctly the next day under the headline:

SYDNEY BUNGLE

Sydney, Friday.

Nothing has been arranged so far in the direction of sending a contingent to China, but it is considered that the requisitioning of the Salamis places the colony under an obligation to send a force. It is contemplated by the Government to submit a proposal to Parliament next week for the despatch of 200 men, and if the vote is passed they will go by the Salamis. The vessel is being fitted up here and will leave for Melbourne next week.

Lyne capitulated and by that evening an informal muster of men of the brigade was informed that their names would have to be sent in by 11 a.m. on Monday if they wished to volunteer for service in China at a rate of pay of 7s 6d per day. The NAV were told the same message, as was the Newcastle Company of the naval brigade. Having had the weekend to think about it, by the time the deadline came just over 100 of the brigade and between 60 and 70 of the Naval Artillery Volunteers had indicated their willingness to serve. This number was within striking distance of the 200 men the government had envisaged and would save the colony from appearing to be unpatriotic in comparison with the other colonies, particularly Victoria.

As the problem of manpower was almost solved, attention now turned to the lamentable state of the brigade's equipment. The intention was to send the contingent as a unit of four companies each with a lieutenant, midshipman, petty officer, leading seaman and 50 men, with a commander in overall command. The men in each company were to be armed with 'the most modern arm', the Lee-Metford rifle, although where these weapons were coming from was not clear. In addition, each company was to have a five-barrelled Nordenfeldt machine gun and a

The Nordenfeldt five-barrelled machine gun was a popular weapon of the mid- to late-nineteenth century. The New South Wales contingent took four guns to China with them. The illustration is probably of the 'Rupertswood Battery' of the Victorian Horse Artillery, whose Commanding Officer in 1885 was Lieutenant Rupert Clarke.

The photograph is probably of the New South Wales Naval Brigade's 9-pounder muzzle-loading cannon, and was taken before the contingent left for China. The Captain of the Gun has his left hand raised to signify that the gun is ready to fire and his right hand holds the firing lanyard. Friction tubes for igniting the propellant charge are probably in the pouch at his waist. The guns were exchanged in Hong Kong for more modern weapons.

In 1900 Captain Francis Hixson had been in command of the New South Wales naval forces since they were first raised in 1863. Three of his sons were lieutenants in the colony's naval forces and a fourth was in the Queensland Naval Brigade.

9-pounder muzzle-loading gun as their heavy weapons. In an effort to explain to a public who might, with some justification, enquire as to the effectiveness of antique muzzle-loading cannon, with a maximum range of 2600 yards, on the 1900 battlefield, the *Telegraph*, in a 'back-grounder', asserted that: 'the 9-pounder was the weapon used by 29 of the 32 ships already on the China Station . . . In fighting a foe armed with the latest type of gun this would probably be a serious drawback, but it is felt that against the Chinese, the great majority of whom are furnished with but primitive weapons, the 9-pounder will prove very effective.' The writer of this article should have been aware through

reading other columns of his paper, that this statement fell somewhat short of the truth, as the Chinese had large quantities of the most modern artillery available.

The problem of accoutrements was to be overcome by calling for the equipment allocated to the Third Contingent for South Africa, dubbed 'England's Last Hope'. Many of the men of this unit had already made their own way to the Cape by working their passages in ships and as a result the government had their unused equipment in Australia. The remaining men, all volunteers, were cooling their heels in Victoria Barracks in the Sydney suburb of Paddington waiting to be formed into small cavalry and

The entire strength of the New South Wales Marine Light Infantry. All were volunteers from the army's Third Contingent to go to South Africa to fight the Boers. They objected to being called 'sailors', and the sailors objected to having 'soldiers' in their ranks, so 'Marine Light Infantry' was a compromise title.

infantry Corps of Instruction.

Command of the contingent was next on the agenda. The venerable Captain Hixson was clearly not in the running in view of his age and lack of experience. His two seconds-in-command, Commander Bosanquet of the NAV and Commander Connor from the naval brigade were possibilities. In the case of the former, and senior, officer, his absolute lack of experience had led to some doubts about his ability to command. Commander Connor, aged 54, was in the same position, not having seen active service for some twenty years. The solution of appointing a younger man would put the New South Wales contingent at a disadvantage vis-a-vis the Victorians with their Commander Tickell, as well as putting Bosanquet's and Connor's noses out of joint.

The whole proposal had first to run the gauntlet of Parliament. Here Lyne faced a good deal of questioning on both the effectiveness of such a small contingent and the fear that to send men away would leave the country defenceless, although these issues appear mutually exclusive. Eventually the Premier was let off the hook — he did have a handsome majority — and the motion was passed. He then sent a cable to this effect to Mr Chamberlain. The reply, when it was received in Sydney, read:

> Her Majesty's Government have received your telegram of 26 July with much pleasure — hired transport Salamis now at Sydney will convey NSW and Victorian contingents to Hong Kong. Force should take with them all guns, rifles and supplies to be exchanged, if possible, on arrival.

The way was at last clear for the first practical steps to be taken towards the enrolment of the New South Wales contingent.

By now the manning proposal had been amended. The contingent would now comprise about 200 naval men and up to 50 men of the permanent infantry and cavalry from the residue of the Third Contingent quartered in Victoria Barracks. It is not clear where the idea of augmenting the force with soldiers arose. Certainly one suspects the hand of Major-General French, the Commandant of the New

South Wales military forces, in the proposal. In the selection of soldiers to join the contingent, preference was to be given to men with seafaring experience. When asked if they would like to go to China the soldiers said they were prepared to go as infantry but objected to being enrolled as naval men. When the naval brigade got to hear about this they strenuously objected to having soldiers in their ranks. Eventually a compromise was reached and the title 'New South Wales Marine Light Infantry' was coined for the soldiers, perhaps modelled on the Royal Marines, who in those days were divided into the Royal Marine Artillery and the Royal Marine Light Infantry. Lieutenant H.E. Lofts was appointed in command of the detachment.

Initial enrolment of the naval members of the contingent took place at the brigade's barracks at Fort Macquarie. First was the medical examination, carried out, according to the *Herald*, 'with wonderful celerity and tact', by the fleet surgeon, Staff Surgeon Steel, and one other doctor. It consisted of a sight test: '. . . reading different sized capital letters backwards and vice versa with two eyes and then with the single orbit at a distance of seven or eight paces'. The candidate '. . . was then ordered to strip to the waist, when he was well sounded and critically inspected and his height and chest measurement taken'. In these circumstances if it not surprising that 'the percentage of rejects was exceedingly small'. The report went on: 'One poor fellow who was desperately anxious to get away, and who looked strong and fit for anything, burst out crying so great was his disappointment at being refused. He pleaded with the two doctors, but whilst they were sympathetic, they were implacable.' In view of the cursory nature of the examination he must have had some very conspicuous medical defect. The deficiency is unlikely to have been a wooden leg as the men had only stripped to the waist.

On passing the medical examination the men were next sworn in for service. The men were all enlisted as able seamen, the question of actual rates being deferred until later, and then turned over to the naval tailors to be measured for their two blue serge suits. They were going to have to make haste with the uniforms. The *Salamis* left Sydney that afternoon for Melbourne and the Victorian contingent was to embark on 31 July. The ship was then due back in Sydney to pick up the New South Welshmen on Friday 3 August, a scant six days off. New South Wales was cutting it very fine indeed.

The thorny question of who was to command the contingent was solved by asking the Admiralty for the loan of a Royal Navy officer to lead them in the field and by placing Commander Connor as second-in-command with the rank of lieutenant (but still wearing the sleeve lace of a commander in the naval brigade). The veteran status of Captain Hixson was recognised by placing him in charge of the contingent for the voyage to Hong Kong. He would then return to Australia. This way, it was felt, the family honour would be preserved. It was already well represented in the contingent, for no fewer than three of his sons, F.W., H.O.N., and A.L., all lieutenants in the naval brigade, had volunteered to go to China. Another son was serving with the Queensland Naval Brigade and did not take part in the expedition.

For their part the Admiralty responded promptly to the request for a field commander and Lieutenant Alexander Gillespie, then serving locally in HMS *Mildura*, was appointed to the post with the rank of captain: in the New South Wales Naval Force it is true, but nevertheless not too bad a promotion.

By 3 August all the officers and men had been selected, partially equipped and allocated to their various companies. The organisation of the New South Wales contingent was thus similar to that of their Victorian counterparts but with the addition of an ambulance company, predominantly stretcher bearers, and the soldiers disguised as the New South Wales Marine Light Infantry. Names of the men of the contingent, keyed to their going-away photographs, are in Appendix II.

For the next few days the newspapers carried several accounts each day of the farewell parties given to the members of the contingent.

Lieutenant H.E. Lofts, commander of the New South Wales Marine Light Infantry which accompanied the naval brigade to China. In the photograph he is wearing the uniform of the 1st Australian Infantry Regiment, which had been his previous unit.

COMMANDER E. R. CONNOR,
Second in Command.

SUB.-LIEUTENANT LINDEMAN.

SUB.-LIEUTENANT SPAIN,
Appointed Lieutenant.

STAFF-SURGEON J. J. STEEL.

LIEUTENANT M. A. ROBERTS, N.A.V.

CAPTAIN FRANCIS HIXSON,
Commanding New South Wales Naval Forces.

LIEUTENANT F. W. HIXSON.

LIEUTENANT H. HIXSON.

MIDSHIPMAN R. CREER,
Appointed Sub-Lieutenant.

MIDSHIPMAN WHITE.

MIDSHIPMAN C. MURNIN.

MIDSHIPMAN BRACEGIRDLE.

EX-CADET L. WALKER,
Appointed Midshipman.

The officers of the New South Wales Naval contingent. The photograph appeared in a popular illustrated weekly of the time The Australian Town and Country Journal. Captain Hixson and one of his sons, Lieutenant G.F.W. Hixson, went only as far as Hong Kong.

Typical was that given to Lieutenant H.O.N. Hixson by his colleagues at the Australian Joint Stock Bank. He received an address and a purse containing 50 sovereigns (presumably from shareholders' funds) as his going-away present. This was the upper end of the social scale. In contrast was the farewell to some of the Balmain members:

> On Saturday night the members of the Mort's Dock Corps of the St John Ambulance Association met at Dick's Hotel, Beattie Street, Balmain, for the purpose of bidding farewell to three members of the corps who are leaving for service in China, viz. Messrs J. M'Farlane, J. Hood and J. Chester. Mr J. Atkins (president) occupied the chair, and there was a large attendance of members and friends. The proceedings were commenced by the singing of the National Anthem.
>
> The chairman, in proposing the health of the departing comrades, said that they were not only well-trained in their particular branch of defence, but were also medallists and certificated men in connection with the Ambulance Corps and Life-saving Society. In concluding, he presented each of the men with a handsome silver-mounted pipe, the gifts of Mr Thomas, an old member of the corps.
>
> Mr M'Farlane responded, and said he felt highly elated at having been selected. He considered the Naval Brigade was one of the finest branches of the service, consisting as it did principally of old navy men. Mr Hood also responded.
>
> A first class musical programme was contributed to by . . .

Messrs G.S. Yuill and Co., then, as now, prominent Sydney importers and exporters, gave their employee, Sub-Lieutenant B. (Bertie) Black, a sword to take with him: 'Mr Black, in returning thanks, said he trusted he would have an opportunity of showing them that he was able to make good use of their very handsome gift.'

A last minute addition to the ranks, and one which came in for carping in Parliament later, were two assistant paymasters. These two men,

John Ross Wallace and George Watkin Wynne, were commissioned into the contingent but in reality they were correspondents for the two leading Sydney newspapers: Wallace for the *Sydney Morning Herald* and Wynne for the *Telegraph*. Their reports were the only link that Australia would have with the contingent. Whether, as members of the contingent, they were paid from public funds as well as collecting their pay as reporters is not known.

The ratings of the New South Wales contingent were very similar in age and background to the men from Victoria. All had seen sea service and over 75 per cent were married. The exceptions were the marines, who were much younger than their naval companions, the majority being in their early twenties.

There was a marked difference in the officers of each contingent. Those from Victoria were mainly warrant officers, having risen from the ranks, and a number of them were ship's officers from HMVS *Cerberus*. Those from New South Wales, reservists to a man, held a commissioned rank and, apart from Commander Connor, lacked experience either as mariners or in command of men at sea or in the field. This apparent difference does not seem to have mattered once the contingents were in China.

Two of the New South Wales officers were somewhat cautious. 'Lambton', recorded Connor in his diary, 'said he would not go as a Sub-Lieutenant as he could not leave a starving wife. Spain wanted 48 hours to consider.' Both went in the end.

As soon as the sailors from both contingents were mustered for active service they became entitled to draw their pay, now settled at 7s 6d a day. The arrangement for them to draw 1s 6d a day while away from Australia, with the balance of 6s going to their families, apparently worked well throughout their absence.

As far as the colonies of Victoria and New South Wales were concerned, contingents had been recruited, sworn in and partially equipped, funds had been provided, transport had been engaged. All was ready for the off.

5

BOUND FROM SOUTH AUSTRALIA

A one-ship navy? Then you are in no danger of collisions in your fleet.
(Remark attributed to the commander of a visiting French cruiser)

THE South Australian Cabinet, it will be recalled, considered the Colonial Secretary's request for the colony's permission to release ships of the Australasian Squadron for service in China on Monday 2 July and cabled their initial response that they 'freely consented'. Later that day they asked the Governor, Lord Tennyson, to send another cable to London offering the British government the use of their entire navy, the warship HMCS *Protector*. The offer of the gunboat was with or without crew and at the expense of the Imperial authorities. Commander Clare, who had recently taken over command of the South Australian naval forces, volunteered to go in command of the gunboat.

By 5 July London had replied to the cable, accepting the offer and enquiring when the ship would be ready to sail. According to the Adelaide *Observer*: 'The reply of the Colonial Office is somewhat obscure, as there is nothing to indicate whether the home authorities desire to have the boat manned by a South Australian crew or not.' The government went ahead, however, and ordered Clare to prepare the ship for sea service in China. The ship's complement was in the region of 100 men, so that in addition to the permanent staff of twelve chief and petty officers, Clare would need to obtain about 90 men from the naval reserve. Fortunately the reserve was in the middle of its annual training and so there was a fairly full muster of men at their drill hall at Largs Bay on Saturday 7 July to hear the naval commandant's call for volunteers.

The first stumbling block appeared before the parade started, when members of the reserve, the majority of whom were, like their counterparts in the other colonies, breadwinners and ex-naval men, asked the obvious question about pay. 'Whose rates are we going on, Imperial or colonial?', thus posing the same question as the men in New South Wales. An able seaman in the South Australian Naval Force was paid 7s a day. Captain Clare solved this problem when he informed the men that the South Australian government had offered to man the gunboat provided that colonial rates of pay were 'conceded', and it was on that understanding that a great number of men stepped forward to give their names to the force's paymaster, Mr Norton.

The flagship of the South Australian Navy, HMCS Protector. *The photograph was probably taken in the Port Adelaide River shortly after her delivery from the United Kingdom in 1884. The cruiser is flying the South Australian colonial flag as an ensign.*

The 6-inch breech-loading quick-firing gun mounted at the stern of HMCS Protector *with the crew at drill. From the left they are: the bugler, to sound the 'open fire' call on his bugle; an ammunition supply number with the propellant charge in a leather holder; the trainer, responsible for training the gun onto the target; another ammunition supply number (who is not smoking, there is a flaw in the photograph), holding a dummy shell with a lanyard so that it can be retrieved from the breech of the gun; a ramming number with, second from the right, a sailor holding the rammer. They will both ram the shell, followed by the charge, into the breech of the gun. Between them, and to the rear, is the firing number with the firing lanyard in his hand, and to his rear is the layer of the gun and the sightsetter. The Captain of the Gun is on the far right of the photograph in blue uniform. Note the absence of footwear.*

The matter of a crew, a list of whom is in Appendix I, having now been solved (provided that the Imperial authorities came to the party about the rates of pay) all that remained was for them to prepare the ship for service in China.

Coal was the most important item to be placed on board. *Protector's* bunkers could only carry enough to steam as far as Sydney before requiring to refuel. After that, coaling stops were planned at Thursday Island, the southern Philippines, Manila and Hong Kong. Fresh water for the boilers and for domestic use would have to be taken on at each port of call as well, for the boilers had no condensers to convert steam produced back into water after it had been used by the engines and as a result it went to waste. Victualling presented no problems, as adequate stocks of food could also be obtained en route.

The chief difficulty appeared to be the ammunition for the ship's main armament. Both the 8-inch and 6-inch guns, although

A view of the after part of the cruiser HMCS Protector *with her crew at action stations manning the after 6-inch gun and the two after Hotchkiss 3-pounders. The photograph was taken just before the ship sailed for China in August 1900 and was published in the* Town and Country Journal.

similar to those in use by the Royal Navy, had been constructed by private enterprise and were not identical to the Imperial pattern. In addition to being somewhat out of date, the ammunition was slightly different to that in Imperial use. The stock of shells for these guns available in South Australia amounted to no more than 200 rounds — whether per gun or in toto is not clear, but the latter is strongly suspected — and after that had been expended in action there would be no more to be had. The variety of shell eventually stowed in *Protector's* shell rooms consisted of steel-armour-piercing, common, Palliser, shrapnel and case. It was assumed that replenishment of powder for propellant charges would be possible from stocks in Hong Kong, and so spare cartridge bags were placed on board for filling there if necessary. A more detailed description of the ammunition is contained in Appendix VI.

Messrs Shierlaw, the government clothing contractors, were, like their New South Wales counterparts, going to have their work cut out. Every man in the crew was to be supplied with two serge jumpers, two pairs of serge trousers, and two flannel shirts. Two jumpers and pairs of trousers in duck, a type of light canvas not dissimilar to modern jeans material, were provided for tropical wear. One guernsey, two collars, two caps and covers and one oilskin coat and sou'wester were also on the crew's clothing list. This naval sartorial bonanza of course included the obligatory cholera belt, a form of broad belt worn round the waist. It was padded over the area of the kidneys at the back, and was considered by the doctors of the time to reduce the chances of the wearer catching cholera. (It was in use in the Royal Navy until the Second World War.)

The ship's captain, Commander Clare, was an ex-merchant marine master who had spent some time in opium steamers running from Calcutta to the Chinese coast. He had been the Commandant of the South Australian Naval

Force and commanding officer of HMCS *Protector* for only a short while. The ship's engineer, Mr W. Clarkson, who held the rank of staff engineer and often wore the uniform of an engineer captain in the force was, by profession, a marine engineer. He was the designer of the ship's engines, had superintended their installation in the United Kingdom, and had sailed with the ship on her delivery voyage. The paymaster, Mr Norton, and chief gunner, the formidable Mr Argent, had both been in the Royal Navy, as had many of the ship's permanent crew.

As far as the crew and public were concerned, the offer of the *Protector* had been made to the mother country and all that was now required was their reply, accepting the offer. This was not quite the whole story, although at the time it appeared to be, if the judicious selection of some of the cables between Adelaide and London was all one had to go on:

> From Secretary of State (S of S) to His Excellency the Governor of South Australia (HEGSA) dated July 5 1900.
>
> In reply to your telegram [offering the *Protector*] I have received with much pleasure the offer of the gunboat. It has been referred to the Admiralty.

From HEGSA to S of S, dated July 7 1900.

> The ship's company consists of captain, two lieutenants, [a] chief gunner, gunner, boatswain, paymaster, 100 petty officers and able seamen, stokers and boys, the staff engineer, the chief engineer, artificer warrant rank, two engineer artificers. The ship must coal every ten days doing ten knots. I presume that the pay will be the same as here — able seamen 7s a day; warrant officers 12s a day; officers the same as in the Royal Navy; as well as pensions for casualties. Can the naval authorities at Sydney be requested to supply magazine rifles, pistols, small arms ammunition, Hotchkiss ammunition and other stores necessary? The Premier has ordered the *Protector* fully armed and equipped, to be ready in ten days. The officers and men most enthusiastic on receipt of orders.

A week later:

> From HEGSA to S of S dated July 12 1900.
>
> The Colonial Government await receipt of answer from the Admiralty as to pay. If colonial rate of pay and allowances *Protector* will start at the beginning of the week; if not, other men must be recruited, causing considerable unavoidable delay.

And four days after that:

> From HEGSA to S of S dated July 16 1900.
>
> Referring to my telegrams of July 7 and 12, the South Australian Government are quite annoyed because no answer has been received as to rate of pay. The *Protector* is quite ready to start today.

From the telegrams above it appeared that the British authorities were dragging their feet. Some degree of blame must be placed on the South Australian shoulders though because they had assumed that London would pay the men at the colonial rate, i.e. 7s a day. Their second telegram implied that if this was not to be the case they would disband the *Protector*'s crew and start all over again with a scratch and untrained set of men. In adopting this attitude the South Australian government had apparently abandoned the principle previously applied to army contingents sent to South Africa, which was that they, not the government in London, paid the difference between the Imperial and colonial rates of pay, thus echoing the attitude of the government of New South Wales.

Faced with what looked suspiciously like blackmail, the British government then offered to make a subsidy for the supply of the *Protector* — whereupon South Australia named an amount which exactly covered the difference between both rates of pay. What could have been an easy way out of what was fast becoming a most unedifying situation was stymied when the British Treasury refused to sanction the subsidy which forced the Secretary of State to decline the services of the *Protector*.

None of the cables covering this haggling were released at the time in Adelaide. As far as

the public was concerned, the next development was:

S of S to HEGSA dated July 28 1900.

Referring to your telegram of July 18, Her
Majesty's Government in present circumstances
regret to be unable to take advantage of the
offer of the use of the *Protector*. They are most
grateful for the readiness evinced by the Colony
to assist at a critical time; and hope that the
decision will not cause inconvenience and
disappointment. If further developments should
make the employment of the *Protector* desirable
they will be glad to avail themselves of it.

Naturally the public reaction in Adelaide when
the message was received and released was one
of anger at the British. The South Australian
cabinet attached a Minute to the telegram and
sent it back to the Governor:

Respectfully returned to His Excellency the
Governor. The Government regret that if this
decision were inevitable it was not communi-
cated at a much earlier date.

The South Australians then went on to point
out that they had already spent £2000 preparing
the *Protector*, and questions were asked in the
House of Assembly as to whether the government was going to ask for a refund from Britain.
On 31 July, Chamberlain sent a cable to
Lord Tennyson saying that he was urging the
Treasury to reconsider. For his part, Tennyson
asked his Ministers to consider more liberal
terms, but they refused.

The stalemate was broken by the Treasury
agreeing to a subsidy of £1000 a month, and a
by-now relieved South Australian government
was able to announce: 'Her Majesty's Government guarantees all expenses.' Those of the
crew who had given up their jobs to join, and

who were voicing their concern about being
able to get them back not having seen service
were satisfied. But after a month's quibbling,
the ship was still not quite ready to sail.

The Admiralty, having accepted the offer of
a warship, were now having second thoughts
about the ship's legal status. This was because
the *Protector*, as a colonial warship, sailed
under the (blue) ensign of the colony of South
Australia, with a pennant flown to indicate that
she was armed. In addition she was not
commanded by a 'proper', i.e. ex-Royal Navy,
officer. This dilemma was eventually solved,
and with the South Australian government's
speedy concurrence it was agreed that the ship
would go as far as Brisbane with Clare in
commanded by a 'proper', i.e. ex-Royal Navy,
Royal Navy officer and the immediate past
commandant of the South Australian Naval
Force, now occupying a similar post in Queensland, would take over command for the deployment, with Clare as senior lieutenant. More-
over, when the ship arrived in Hong Kong she
would re-commission into the Royal Navy as
HMS *Protector* and accordingly fly the White
Ensign. The officers would receive commissions,
the warrant officers warrants and the men would
be signed on as ratings in the navy.

The naval services of three of the four
colonies who had initially offered to help the
mother country were now ready for departure.
All that was outstanding was the outcome of
the Queensland offer of their gunboats *Paluma*
or *Gayundah*. The British government, presumably with the benefit of numerous con-
fidential reports as to the efficiency of the
Queensland Marine Defence Force, eventually
replied thanking the government but rejecting
both ships because they were both 'too old and
too slow'.

6

OFF TO WAR

It was fortunate for the impatient and well-equipped Victorians, though considerably less so for the foot-dragging New South Wales government and their ill-equipped naval brigade, that the problem of getting their men to China was solved with the engagement of the SS *Salamis* as a transport. She had arrived in Melbourne in the evening of 10 July, coming from London via the Cape, where she had taken on board several Australian military invalids from the Boer War.

The steamer, an Aberdeen Line cargo passenger ship, was on the Admiralty's list of ships suitable for use as troop transports and on arrival in Sydney from Melbourne she was requisitioned, becoming Her Majesty's *Transport 105*. A.H.H. Douglas, her captain, was a lieutenant in the Royal Naval Reserve, and her crew would don the uniforms of the Reserve when the ship went into Imperial government service.

The gap in the company's regular liner run between Australia, the Cape and London was filled by advancing the sailing date of the next of the company's fleet, the *Aberdeen*. The *Salamis*, at 4650 tons, had been built in 1898 and was the pride of George Thompson's Aberdeen White Star fleet. She was a handsome ship, retaining a graceful clipper bow and barquentine rig to take advantage of fair winds. The dark green paint of the hull was offset by a white superstructure and a yellow funnel. Her economical service speed was in the order of twelve knots.

Having unloaded her cargo from Europe she bunkered with coal at Pyrmont and was then moved to an anchorage off Garden Island for conversion to a transport. This required a minimum amount of work, largely involving the rigging of hammock bars in the 'tween-deck holds to accommodate 500 men and the provision of some tables and chairs. The officers were to be berthed in the normal passenger cabins while the chief and petty officers were to be quartered in the poop deck spaces.

The Victorians continued to niggle. The Premier sent a telegram to the Senior (Royal) Naval Officer Port Jackson urging that in view of the plague in Sydney the ship should be stored and victualled in Melbourne. This elicited the almost accurate response: 'There is no danger from the plague, it is practically extinct here', thus ending that particular attempt at colonial pork-barrelling. Another short-lived problem arose when some of the ship's firemen and stewards went on strike for higher wages because the ship had been taken out of her normal run and was heading off on government duty. This move was halted by the prompt mustering of the crew by Captain Douglas for an address by Captain Royle from the Royal Navy. Remarks such as 'taking very short measure' and the threat of 'severe penalties', coupled with the discharge of four of the men who had just been signed on, brought the crew to heel and the ship was able to sail for Melbourne on 28 July fully coaled and victualled for the voyage to China.

The Victorian contingent at their depot at Williamstown before embarking on the troopship Salamis. *This is one of the field gun's crews. Another photograph of the contingent is in Appendix III.*

The well-organised Victorians were mobilised and sworn in on Saturday 23 July at the Williamstown barracks. After collecting their kit and making arrangements for the disposition of their pay, they were ferried out to HMVS *Cerberus* to live on board the monitor until their departure, tentatively planned for 30 July, the day after the arrival of the *Salamis*. The interim would be spent ashore in field drill and such other training that might come in handy.

Salamis arrived alongside the Breakwater Pier, Williamston, on Sunday 29 July. The work of embarking the heavy stores, guns and limbers started at once, and was completed that evening.

On Monday 30 July the contingent embarked, not, as one might have thought, directly across the quay, but by a more circuitous and cumbersome route. Having landed from HMVS *Cerberus* at Williamstown, the contingent boarded a special train (which cost, according to the Victorian Defence Department Accounts, £5 0s 0d) and were taken the eight or so miles into Melbourne to the Spencer Street station, arriving about noon. They then

detrained and set off from Spencer Street, passing along Collins Street to Parliament House. Here they were addressed by the Lieutenant Governor and the Premier in suitable terms and doubtless at suitable length. After Commander Tickell had called for three cheers for both dignitaries, the contingent moved off, retracing their steps through South Melbourne to Port Melbourne, where they embarked on a tug to take them out to the *Salamis*, which had shifted berth slightly and was now lying off the end of the pier and taking on ammunition.

En route, as one newspaper account coyly said:

. . . the roadway was lined with excited crowds. Numbers of people ran out to the men with uncorked bottles as the procession moved through the suburbs, and much more of this kind of refreshment was offered than would have sufficed merely to quench their thirst. The relatives of the men had gathered for the final farewells, and they were so persistent in their claims on the men that the contingent, which had approached the multitude in proper

Captain Tickell and the officers of the Victorian contingent. In every photograph available, Tickell has the jacket of his uniform buttoned up the 'wrong' way, i.e. right over left.

marching formation, now became thoroughly disorganised.

All was eventually sorted out, and the embarkation was completed by 4.00 p.m., one of the final events being the presentation by the YMCA of a New Testament to each of the contingent. At 4.15 p.m. *Salamis* weighed anchor and got underway. As she made downstream many of the Victorian bluejackets climbed into the rigging to wave farewell. 'These [the crowds] remained watching the transport and the *Cerberus*, which accompanied the transport down the Bay, until the two vessels offered no other object to the eye than some faint discolourations of smoke against the grey wintry sky in the direction of the Heads.'

After this heartrending description of the departure, it is perhaps an anticlimax to report that *Salamis* anchored for the night just over the horizon, off Dromana, passing through Port Phillip Heads the next morning before setting course for Sydney. The *Herald* described her arrival in Port Jackson on Saturday 4 August:

The *Salamis* looked very handsome as she emerged yesterday morning from the fog and came up the harbour. With the sun shining upon her shapely green-painted hull the troopship formed a striking picture when she rounded to and shackled to the flagship buoy off Farm Cove ... The arrangements are now strictly up to naval discipline ... At the gangway a smartly dressed quartermaster meets the would-be visitor, asks for his card, and after a while the visitor is ushered on deck ...

The band of the Victorian Navy accompanied the contingents to China. It was a composite of the Permanent Services and the Naval Brigade.

There was a decided warlike air abroad throughout the vessel, and over the magazine there paraded a sentry armed with a repeater. The able seamen of the ship, who are dressed in the blue of the Royal Naval Reserve, saluted as they passed along the upper decks, while below, the Victorians, upon whose caps were written HMS [sic] *Cerberus*, performed a similar naval duty as their superiors passed through the quarters.

The New South Wales contingent was making frantic last minute arrangements. The composition of the naval brigade had been finalised only in the middle of the previous week, with the marines being sworn in as late as Saturday 4 August, the day the *Salamis* arrived in Sydney. The naval component had moved into barracks at Fort Macquarie the previous Wednesday and much of the time was taken up with equipping the force with arms and uniforms. The date for embarkation was set for Tuesday 7 August. The heavy equipment was to be loaded, as was the case with the Victorians, the day before, after the *Salamis* had shifted to an alongside berth at Woolloomooloo.

Social events farewelling members of the contingent, culminated on Monday 6 August in a smoking concert for them and their new chums from Victoria at the Sydney Town Hall. Events started at 8.00 p.m. and appear to have consisted mainly of musical items. The Mayor arrived two hours after the programme began and in his speech he said he looked forward to welcoming them on their return. One of the

The Town Hall in Sydney was the venue for a smoking concert for both contingents before they sailed for China. The Mayor arrived two hours late for the festivities.
This is the first in a number of illustrations in the book which are taken from glass-plate negatives taken by Staunton Spain, who went to China as a lieutenant in the New South Wales contingent.

men was unable to make the festivities. Able Seaman Hart fell off a tram and broke his ankle and was unable to sail with the contingent.

At 3.00 p.m. on embarkation day the contingent mustered in the drill hall at Fort Macquarie in heavy marching order with fixed bayonets and cutlasses drawn. A great deal of handshaking was going on as the politicians of the day did their best to get mentioned in the press. On a blackboard in the room was chalked a notice:

> We are now under the Naval Discipline Act. Officers and men will shave in accordance therewith.

This meant that those who did not wear both a moustache and a beard were required to discard the former. As mature men at that time often wore moustaches only, this resulted in the transformation of many of them.

At about 3.45 p.m. the order to fall in was given and the parade formed up, moving off shortly after. At their head was Captain Hixson, in an open carriage, preceded by five or six mounted police to clear the way. They marched up Macquarie Street, past the Sydney Hospital and Royal Mint, then turned by St Mary's Cathedral towards Woolloomooloo, arriving alongside the *Salamis* at Cowper Wharf at 4.30 p.m. and marching straight on board.

Fifteen minutes later the ship was shifted to moorings in the harbour, where she would have to remain for 24 hours in accordance with an Admiralty instruction, the purpose of which

The New South Wales contingent leaving their Drill Hall at Fort Macquarie and setting off on their march to Woolloomooloo at about 4.00 p.m. on Tuesday 7 August 1900. The photograph is taken from what is now the forecourt of the Opera House.

is long-forgotten. Apart from a contretemps caused by the *Salamis's* Chief Steward committing suicide by shooting himself in the throat the night passed quietly.

Next day the contingents were visited by local dignitaries: the Governor, Lord Beauchamp, and Sir William Lyne, who must have been breathing a sigh of relief that the men had actually got on board more or less on time, and in comparatively good order. Both gave comprehensive addresses to the contingents. And as if that wasn't enough, in the afternoon there was a further visitation, this time by the Minister of Defence, the Minister for Lands, his Principal Under-Secretary and the Under-Secretary for Works.

The New South Wales contingent's mascot Nipper, with a Fort Macquarie gun as a background. The dog was presented to the contingent by Lieutenant Thompson.

Transport 105, *alias SS Salamis, leaving Cowper Wharf in the afternoon of 7 August 1900 for an anchorage in Farm Cove before sailing the next day for China. Members of the Victorian contingent are decorating the foremast.*

Immediately before sailing, in a classic 'pier-head jump', one of Lieutenant Loft's marines fell sick and it was decided to land him. A boatload of his erstwhile colleagues was lying off the *Salamis* waiting to wave farewell. A volunteer to replace the sick man was called for, at which all in the boat called 'We'll come!' Eventually Private Ferns was selected. His name does not appear in the illustrations in Appendix II for this reason.

Finally, in the words of the *Herald*:

> ... the steam winch was set going on the cable, though the ship was hove short long before ... the *Salamis* then blew her final sonorous blast as the anchor hove in sight. She then steamed up the harbour a bit and went round on her port helm, the boys in khaki and in blue being up in the rigging, and the [Victorian Navy's] band played the National Anthem. As a westerly squall came down she rounded Bradley's Head, and in half an hour was outside the waters of Port Jackson on her way to China.

The New South Wales contingent were quartered in the forward holds of the Salamis. *In this photograph some are going down on to the for'rard welldeck from the superstructure, just having embarked in the late afternoon of 7 August 1900. The Victorians had been allocated the after holds as their accommodation.*

Another photograph of the Salamis *leaving Cowper wharf at Woolloomooloo with both contingents on board. On the voyage to Hong Kong, sails were set on the foremast to increase the ship's speed.*

In South Australia two days previously, on Monday 6 August, the *Adelaide Observer* had reported:

> ... precisely at 4 o'clock Captain Clare and his navigating officer, Lieutenant Weir, mounted the bridge, the stern moorings were let go, and the ship, now fairly aglow with the cheers of enthusiastic and earnest seamen, swung round with her head downstream, to the accompaniment of shouts from thousands of throats and the waving of thousands of handkerchiefs and miniature flags by the assembled sightseers ... 'Slow Ahead' was telegraphed to the engine room. The first wash from the twin screws was the signal for renewed cheering and the services of the crew no longer being required on deck all hands swarmed up the rigging, and there answered cheer by cheer.
>
> Abreast of the Torpedo Station a touching and pretty little incident was observed. As the

Protector steamed past, a daughter of Petty Officer Perry, who is an expert in the art of semaphore signalling, waved the message 'Good-bye, dad,' and the rest of the family waved handkerchiefs. Perry had been waiting for this last farewell and he replied 'Good-bye, and God bless you.' One of the flags he was using slipped from his grasp into the water. His disappointment at the mishap was plainly discernible on his face, though, sailor-like, he laughed it off.

On board were two able seamen who were friends — George Frederick Jeffery and John Henry Gill (later Lieutenant Commander). The former kept a diary, which he eventually gave to his friend. Gill died in 1972 at the age of 92. He is thought to have been the oldest survivor of the crew. Jeffery's diary provides the details of part of the story of the *Protector*'s deployment, as do the reminiscences of Captain (later Rear-

HMCS Protector *on the point of sailing from Adelaide on her voyage to northern China. There is a large crowd of well-wishers on shore and in several small boats. The slip rope is rove and the ship's signal letter flags are ready to be broken at the port yard.*

Admiral Sir) William Rooke Creswell and the somewhat mysterious Chief Gunner Blake, who joined the ship as a special service officer and interpreter in Townsville on her way north.

Protector steamed into Port Jackson later in the evening of 10 August — a scant 48 hours after the *Salamis* had left with the New South Wales and Victorian contingents. 'The good ship', said the *Herald* the next day, '. . . is bound upon her worthy mission of upholding the name of the Land of the Golden Fleece . . . and prove to the world the loyalty of Australia's sons.'

Protector would conduct a completely separate campaign and would never meet the rest of the Australians while they were in China.

7

'FIRST TURN OF THE SCREW
CANCELS ALL DEBTS'

For the first day out from Sydney, Her Majesty's *Transport 105*, alias *Salamis*, remained in sight of the New South Wales coast, making 12 knots in a SW 'hard breeze', and was reported by the Smokey Cape lighthouse at 3.30 in the afternoon of the 9th August as signalling 'all's well'. In response the lighthouse used signal flags to send the message 'Farewell to Australia'. By then the contingent had settled down into their new quarters, the New South Welshmen in the forward 'tween decks and the Victorians aft. The saloon and cabins amidships were, of course, taken by the officers. In view of the antecedents of the men of the contingents, it is more than probable that there were many 'old ships' tales to be told, for a great many of the men had not only served in the Royal Navy but had spent time in China waters. Even the marines, youngsters as the majority were, boasted one who had seen service in the Cuban war and another who claimed to have had numerous hairsbreadth escapes from Apaches and other wild Red Indian tribes as a Texas scout. It was enough to scare the living daylights out of a young sailor or marine away from mum for the first time. Taking departure from the Australian coast, the ship headed across the Coral Sea, setting the fore topsail, fore t'gallant and fore trysail, making landfall in the vicinity of Cape Deliverance at the southeast extremity of New Guinea. It was here in 1857 that a shipload of Chinese coolies on their way to the gold fields of Australia had been shipwrecked, with about 150

of their number being captured, fattened and then eaten by the locals. Or so that old salt Commander Connor said, claiming to have heard the story from a French survivor. Smooth seas, but it was getting warmer, and the haste of the arrangements for the New South Wales contingent became apparent, for they had sailed without tropical uniforms. They were not very comfortable.

Life on board followed a routine that must have appeared relaxed to those who had served before in the Royal Navy. Hammocks had to be lashed up and stowed by 7.00 a.m., breakfast being served fifteen minutes later. Colours (the daily raising of the ensign) were at 8.00 a.m. After a general clean-up, Divisions followed at 9.20 with prayers being read by the two commanding officers in turn. Rounds were carried out daily at 11.00 a.m. and 9.00 p.m., with pipe-down at 10.00 p.m. Colours were hoisted to the accompaniment of the National Anthem from the Victorians' brass band, probably under the baton of Petty Officer Walter Underwood. The band also earned its keep by playing every morning and evening on the bridge deck. Small arms, machine gun and gun drill was carried out as frequently as was practicable. The New South Wales Ambulance Party, with their somewhat ambivalent role, were exercised at both bandaging and cutlass drill (using their bayonets). Vaccinations against smallpox, using 'lymph' from the Sydney Health Board collected prior to sailing, were soon carried out.

Sunday 12 August saw the issue of the first

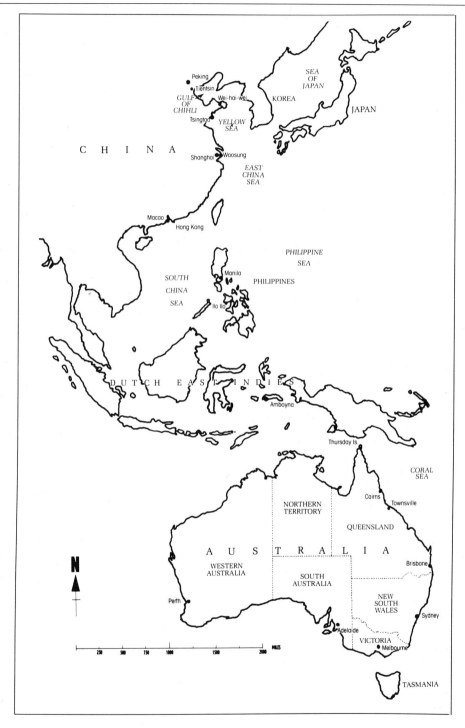

Western Pacific Ocean showing major ports of call for SS Salamis and HMCS Protector.

Transport 105 *made about 12 knots on her voyage to Hong Kong from Sydney.*

edition of the ship's paper *Salamis Screecher*, from the joint pens of assistant paymasters cum journalists Wynne and Wallace. Copies were 2s 6d each. There is no record of the disposal of the proceeds.

Once clear of the north coast of New Guinea, the next event to occupy the contingent was the 'Crossing the Line' ceremony, performed for members of the crew or passengers who were crossing the Equator for the first time. On the *Salamis* one of the ship's company appeared on the forecastle on 16 August, the day the Equator was crossed, dressed as King Neptune, festooned with seaweed and barnacles, with a golden crown of cardboard and a flowing beard made of oakum. He was accompanied, according to Wallace, by his wife, 'Queen' Amphitrite, a 'bishop', a scrofulous barber and surgeon, and several 'guards', 'nymphs' and 'bears'. The procession made its way round the ship, finally arriving at a large canvas bath rigged over one of the fore-hatches and filled with sea water.

One by one the acolytes, 'debutantes' in Loft's words, were led, protesting, in front of Neptune (Petty Officer Fitzpatrick, 'looking like

a Viking statue'), who, brandishing his trident, soundly berated them before handing them over to the tender ministrations of the barber, who covered them with a foul-tasting and smelling lather made of soft soap and grease, and then to the surgeon, who proceeded to shave them with a large wooden razor, followed by the 'bears' who gave the victim a thorough soaking in the bath: a good opportunity for wild horse-play and the paying-off of old scores. Eventually the victims were released and given a certificate testifying to their having joined King Neptune's kingdom. The certificates became prized partly for their historic merit but mainly as an insurance against repetition of the ordeal. Wallace's remains, in his diary.

Transport *Salamis*   EQUATOR
                              147 East Longitude
                              16th August 1900

NEPTUNE'S PASSPORT

This is to certify that I, NEPTUNUS REX, have this Day Baptized into the ALMIGHTY KINGDOM OF THE DEEP, *Asst. Paymaster*

Crossing the line ceremony on board Salamis. *In the photographs the Doctor/barber, King Neptune and the Bishop are doing their duties initiating newcomers into the mysteries of the ritual. The tank rigged over a hatchcover in which the unfortunates were finally submerged is also seen with one occupant at the end of his ordeal.*

J.R. Wallace who, hereafter, and for ALL TIME, shall have full Liberty and Licence to sail where-soe'r he listeth.

> Given under my hand and SEAL
>
> (Neptunus Rex)

Witness (A.H.H. Douglas)
Captain S.S. *Salamis*

Commander Connor didn't care for the ceremony at all. He had crossed the line on numerous previous occasions and so was given a 'bye', but to be on the safe side he collected and stored his certificate.

North of the Equator, the ship came under the influence of the south-west monsoon and the calm weather turned to a moderate gale. This played havoc not only with the young marines, but also with those suffering from the effects of the vaccinations they had received two or three days before. Cape Engano, the northernmost part of Luzon Island, was rounded on Friday 24 August and course was set, in calm but hot and muggy weather, for Hong Kong. The average speed for the passage from Sydney had been about 12 knots.

As the South China coast drew closer there must have been considerable apprehension in the minds of many on board. The *Salamis* had not met with any other sail on the seventeen-day voyage from Sydney and was not fitted with Signor Marconi's apparatus. In 1900 that was reserved for the flagships of the world's navies so there was no way of knowing the situation in China.

8

CATCHING UP

After the *Salamis* arrived in Hong Kong, entering harbour through Lye-mun on the morning of Sunday 26 August and anchoring off Victoria at 9.30 a.m., the most pressing requirement for those on board was news of the beleaguered, indeed probably massacred, legations in Peking. Fragmentary reports had appeared in the Sydney papers before they had left that a second, larger, international relief force had set off from Tientsin, but news of its success, or, in view of the alarming tales about the involvement of the Chinese Army, perhaps its lack of success, were a matter of prime importance.

The first news received was that the inhabitants of the legations had been relieved, on 14 August, by a mixed force of approximately 20 000 men led by a British general, Gaselee. The numbers of troops provided by each country participating were:

Japanese	about 10 000
Russians	4 000
British	3 000
Americans	2 000
French	800
Germans	100
Austrians	100

As far as the author is aware, this was the first time that an allied force, i.e. one involving troops from several nations with a single commander, had been formed. The force had left Tientsin after what appears, with 84 years of hindsight, to have been an inexcusable delay of more than six weeks. This was justified at the time because, as far as anyone knew, the purpose of the expedition — to relieve the staffs and families of the various legations — had been negated by their supposed deaths. It would be better, and more prudent, to wait until the force was strong enough to take on the task of retribution with every chance of success.

Following his defeat at the hands of the Chinese, Seymour had withdrawn to the arsenal north of Tientsin to wait for reinforcements. This had proved to be a somewhat lengthy spell, as there were none to be had. Not until the arrival of HMS *Terrible* from Hong Kong with a regiment of British soldiers, plus a Russian troopship from Vladivostok with some Russian infantry, could a further force be landed from the ships off Taku to go to his aid. While waiting for these reinforcements the forts at Taku had been secured. They guarded the entrance to the Pei Ho, the river that led up to Tientsin, and the railway line that led from Shan-hai-kwan, through Tangku, on the north bank of the river opposite Taku, thence through Tientsin to the capital.

The forts were stormed on 17 June. Simultaneously two modern Royal Navy destroyers, HMShips *Fame* and *Whiting*, captured four German-built Chinese Navy destroyers which were lying in a small base just inshore of the forts. By capturing the Taku forts, it was possible to land the troops which were now appearing on board ships of the various Powers in the Gulf of Chihli. By the beginning of August

HMS Whiting, *shown here in dry dock, was one of two Royal Navy destroyers which had captured four Chinese destroyers at their base near the fort at Taku.* Whiting, *with a top speed of about 30 knots, was one of the first of the new type of ship called torpedo boat destroyers from their role, which was to protect the capital ships of the fleet from attack by small, fast, torpedo boats.*

some 25 000 men were under arms in the Tientsin area, and following the arrival of the British Commander-in-Chief, General Gaselee, the majority of them had set off for Peking on 4 August.

After a comparatively short and easy campaign Peking had been relieved on 14 August, the first troops to enter the legation quarter being Sikhs and Rajputs from the Indian Army who, under their British officers, had gained admittance by breaking through the gate which secured the main sewer.

Following the raising of the siege the Chinese court, to all intents and purposes embodied in the person of the Empress Dowager Tz'u-hsi, had fled to the west, and both the Imperial Chinese Army and the Boxers seemed to have disappeared into thin air.

At a conference held in Peking, two courses of action had been considered. Some of the Allies were in favour of appeasement of the Chinese, arguing that the advent of the Boxers was, to a degree, a one-off phenomenon and that to carry out reprisals would be against the interests of future relations between the Chinese government and the West. Other nations, particularly the Germans, who had a large expeditionary force still on the high seas steaming at full speed for a war which was now over, argued, understandably, that reprisals were the order of the day. In the end the appeasers won, to the intense disappointment of the Germans.

The threat of a resurgence of the Boxer hordes was still uppermost in everyone's minds

The remains of the French section of the Legation quarter of Peking after the siege had been lifted. Most of it had been abandoned by the defenders as the Chinese pressed their attacks home.

as was the fear that the uprising might still spread to other parts of the country, but that likelihood seemed to be reducing as the days went by. Even so, at the time the *Salamis* arrived in Hong Kong, the future course of events was by no means clear.

While absorbing this state of affairs, the officers and men of the Australian contingents were busy arming themselves for the campaigns that might yet still lie ahead. The Royal Navy authorities in Hong Kong decided that, in the cause of standardisation, the contingents' miscellany of weapons be exchanged for standard Imperial issue models during the time the Australians were to be in China. The plan was to loan the weapons in Hong Kong from their stores there and collect them on the contingents' way back to Australia. Accordingly, the New South Wales contingent's earlier pattern Lee-Metford Mk II magazine rifles with the 'modern' bayonets (borrowed from the Royal Navy in Sydney and issued on the way up to Hong Kong) and the Victorians' less satisfactory and even older Martini-Enfield rifles with triangle bayonets were all turned in. In exchange they were issued with the newer Lee-

Metford Mk II* rifles and associated equipment. Machine guns were standardised on the .45-inch Maxim, the antique Nordenfeldts from New

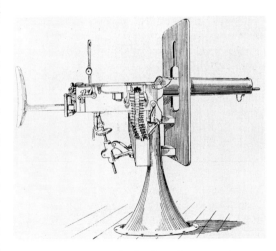

The contingents standardised on the .45-inch Maxim machine gun by drawing several from the Royal Navy stores in Hong Kong. The guns came equipped with a wheeled carriage for use on land as well as the shipboard mounting shown here. More details of the weapons used are in Appendix VII.

South Wales being handed in.

Finally, the field guns of both contingents were exchanged for the modern naval 12-pounder quick-firing guns mounted on land carriages. The guns came supplied with limbers and ammunition waggons. These 12-pounders had recently achieved fame throughout the Empire when they had been landed from ships of the Royal Navy in South Africa and had accompanied the (Royal) Naval Brigade on their march as part of the column that relieved Ladysmith. Details of some of the weapons associated with the contingents, both in Australia and in the field, are contained in Appendix VII.

The New South Wales contingent attempted to obtain some form of wheeled transport, as they had omitted, or forgotten, to bring any with them from Sydney. They were unsuccessful in their endeavours. The smug Victorians had come supplied with waggons for their sick, stores and baggage.

On Tuesday 28 August the *Salamis* was visited by the Commodore-in-Charge, Hong Kong, Commodore Powell, who inspected the men of the two contingents and made complimentary remarks. His inspection was brief, which was probably just as well for the men wearing their heavy blue uniforms in late summer in Hong Kong.

The Victorians had had the foresight to bring a supply of khaki material with them — bought for 2s 3d a yard — and were going to utilise the Hong Kong tailors, renowned even then for their marvels of instant workmanship. In the event even they couldn't fill the demand and the uncut khaki went north with the Victorians.

The command of the New South Wales contingent now passed into the hands of Lieutenant (acting Captain, New South Wales Naval Brigade) Gillespie, who then became the senior officer of both colonial units. Captain Hixson, his staff officer (and son) Lieutenant G.F. Hixson, his steward Able Seaman Poole, and four able seamen from the New South Wales contingent, medically unfit despite their 'rigorous examination' in Sydney, all left the ship for HMS *Tamar*, the former line-of-battle ship now lying in the harbour as an accommodation hulk, thence to return to Australia on board the SS *Airlie*. Leave was given to both watches of the men while in Hong Kong. Their liberty was preceded with the issue of a month's pay. Only one libertyman was in trouble — for drunkenness.

Reports of the Australians' arrival in China must by this time have percolated up to the British Commander-in-Chief, General Gaselee, now installed in Peking, for the next day, 29 August, they were ordered to sail in the *Salamis*, via Shanghai, for the north, to be landed at Taku. Both contingents were to be brigaded (a phrase then current in military circles meaning to form one unit) as part of the First Brigade, British Contingent, China Field Force.

When the Boxer uprising had erupted, the only British forces available had been the sailors and marines serving on board ships of the China Station. Following the defeat of Admiral Seymour and his force, it had become imperative to supply many more troops to relieve the legations and restore order or exact retribution. Britain clearly had a major role to play in any international punitive expedition to be mounted by the Powers affected by the uprising. However, as she was over-extended in South Africa in her war with the Boers, the only troops readily available were those of her Indian Army.

By the time the Australians arrived in Hong Kong, the preponderance of British troops, some 9000, were from Indian Army regiments and ancillary units. The only Imperial troops in the field in North China were a battalion of the Royal Welsh Fusiliers and a battery of the Royal Horse Artillery. Both had been part of the garrison of Hong Kong, and the Governor and Commander-in-Chief there could be expected, in view of the possibility of a widespread Chinese anti-foreigner insurrection, to want them back.

The supposed lessons of the Indian Mutiny, coupled with the fact that the other major participants in the Allied force were all using troops of their own blood, must have made the presence of the unarguably British-looking

The main entrance to the Taku fort in 1900. It was proposed to billet the Victorians in this mud-brick fort for their time in China. The accommodation consisted of small, damp, dark rooms overrun with vermin.

Australians more than welcome to the commander of the British contingent. This probably more than compensated for the fact that they had no experience in the field. The day before they left Hong Kong, though, the German contingent arrived hot foot from Europe. This expeditionary force, under the command of a Supreme Commander in the shape of Field Marshal Count Alfred von Waldersee, was lusting for battle and its associated glory. The Australians were to experience some of the consequences of this attitude in the weeks ahead.

The newly exchanged 12-pounders and Maxim machine guns were put on board the *Salamis* on Thursday 30 August and the ship left Hong Kong early the next morning, coasting north-eastwards along the Fukien coast of China. The morning of the third day out, Steep Island was passed close on the port beam, giving some of those on deck a mild scare. Soon afterwards the pilot boarded and the ship made its way to the anchorage off the Woosung Bar, at the mouth of the Yangtze Kiang. On arrival both commanding officers, Captain Gillsepie and Commander Tickell, left the *Salamis* to call on Admiral Seymour, who was visiting Shanghai

in his dispatch vessel HMS *Alacrity*. On their return to the ship that evening they announced that the contingents would be employed in North China, in all probability garrisoning the forts at Taku.

Although they put a bold face on it, this was a bitter disappointment. The Taku forts were known to be particularly uncomfortable and, in addition, it looked as if the action would be going on elsewhere. This gloomy forecast was borne out by the Senior Naval Officer Woosung, Captain Clarke, Royal Navy. He visited *Salamis* the next morning before the ship sailed in order to inspect the contingents and to report on the balance of the ship's charter. Clarke addressed the men:

It is a beastly fort, and Taku is a beastly place, but you must wait patiently ... Knowing China very well I would like to warn you about two things. The first is, do not drink the water; and the second is, beware of all vegetables which grow above ground such as lettuce. They must not be eaten, or you will be troubled with worms and rendered unfit for duty ... Remember you are doing good work for Queen and country. They call you the Australian Contingent — that was a very good name —

59

but remember this — we all regard you as the British Contingent from Australia.

(Cheers)

His dispatch read:

Inspection of Australian Contingent

HMS 'Undaunted' at Wusung,
4th September 1900

Sir,

I have the honour to report that in accordance with your orders I visited the transport *Salamis* on the 4th instant and inspected the Australian contingent.

I have never seen a finer body of men, they are clean and smart looking.

Our country is fortunate in having so many staid and disciplined men (many of them old men of war's men) willing to volunteer for active service.

I understand that more may be had if required.

I have etc.
(Sd) A.C. CLARKE
Captain

Vice Admiral
SIR EDWARD H. SEYMOUR, K.C.B.
Commander-in-Chief

By the time the good Captain had returned to his ship, *Salamis* should have been hull-down on the horizon bound for Taku but was still at anchor, having missed the tide. The ship finally got underway on the morning of 5 September.

The British base of Wei-hai-wei was reached on the morning of 7 September but, as the ship was departing the next day for Taku, leave was restricted to officers and chief petty officers. Britain had obtained possession of Wei-hai-wei from the Japanese who, having bombarded and then occupied the port during the Sino–Japanese war of 1894–95, had evacuated it under the terms of the Cheefoo Convention of 1897. Its main advantage to the British was as a coaling station and as a place in the cooler north to which servicemen and their wives could escape the hot and humid Hong Kong summer. During the three years the British had been in occupation they had made some

improvements, the most important being a 500-bed field hospital where about 200 beds were now occupied by wounded sailors and soldiers from the campaign in northern China, with more arriving daily. These casualties were not as much a result of the fighting, which by now had largely died away, as of the enteric fever and dysentery which were fast becoming epidemic amongst the Allied troops in northern China. Also in harbour was the United States hospital ship *Maine*, which had been fitted out at the instigation of Lady Randolph Churchill for service in South Africa.

On the morning of 8 September *Salamis* weighed anchor for the last 240-mile leg of her voyage from Australia to the war front. After an uneventful short run across the Gulf of Chihli from Wei-hai-wei, she joined the great fleet of warships of various nations which had assembled twelve to fifteen nautical miles off the mouth of the Hai Ho. This distance off shore was because of the shallow water over the bar of the river. *Salamis* anchored near the flagship, the British battleship HMS *Barfleur*, on Sunday September 9 in the middle of the fleet, estimated as having a strength of 130 warships and transports of all classes and sizes. The contingents' arrival was, once again, unexpected by the staff responsible for the disposition of the daily increasing number of military men from eight countries, now assembling as a second field force. The first and most urgent problem was that of shore accommodation for the Australians. The *Salamis* was due to sail for the south in a few days with detachments of Royal Marines now withdrawn from the China Field Force to rejoin their ships in Hong Kong. Rear Admiral Bruce's initial solution was for the Victorian contingent to be installed in one of the Taku forts and for the New South Wales force to go to Peking and find accommodation there.

An inspection of the fort was made on Monday 10 September by the commanding officers of the two contingents, accompanied by the *Salamis's* Captain Douglas. They made their way ashore in one of the captured Chinese torpedo boats, renamed HMS *Taku* by her new owners, the Royal Navy, and before landing at

One of four Chinese torpedo boat destroyers captured by the Royal Navy at Taku and renamed Taku, *and lying alongside the British battleship HMS* Centurion. *The other three ships were presented to Russia, Germany (who had built them for the Chinese and had only just delivered them) and France.*

the fort first made their way some miles up-stream to deliver mail to the gunboat HMS *Algerine.*

The fort, one of four then existing at the mouth of the river, presented an unprepossessing edifice to the inspection team. Everything — walls, roof, floors — was built of mud. The structure was rectangular in shape, with sides of about 1200 feet. The outer wall, about 30 feet high, with a thickness at its base of about 20 feet tapering to 10 feet at the top, was

The Taku forts 1984. The Chinese Navy use what remains of the forts as a small signal station with two or three sailors in residence. View taken from the north bank of the Hai Ho, which becomes the Pei Ho as it nears the sea.

surrounded by moats, with a few narrow cause-ways leading to the mainland. The proposed accommodation consisted of small, damp, dark rooms overrun with vermin. The prospect of spending time in these gloomy conditions was, understandably, not at all appealing to the Victorians, and it was therefore with relief that amending orders were received the next day. The staff in Peking had decided that the Australian brigade was now to be quartered as one force in Tientsin. Arrangements were put in hand to land all the equipment and men by large lighters under the tow of tugs. The lighters were loaded on 14 September and the men left the *Salamis* at daybreak on the 15th.

The original plan was that the force should be landed a few miles upstream from the mouth of the river at the British supply base at Sin Ho and go as far as they were able towards Tientsin by train. This was because reports had been received by General Gaselee's staff in the capital that large numbers of Chinese troops and Boxers were concentrating in the vicinity of Tientsin. These reports were accepted and amplified by Admiral Bruce, who was convinced that fighting was actually going on around Tientsin when he directed the Australians there.

Bruce was, by this time, getting his information from Peking partly through the use of the brand new Marconi system of wireless telegraphy, reports being first relayed by landline from the capital to an installation set up in one of the forts and then transmitted the fifteen miles to the flagship. The equipment was in the hands of an expert with the rank of Gunner and 'up till sundown the instrument works splendidly, but at night it is absolutely unreliable'. All the German warships were equipped with Signor Marconi's instruments, a fact which had come as a surprise to the Royal Navy.

The news of the imminent action spurred the contingent into activity. As Our Special Correspondent said' in his dispatch to the *Telegraph*:

> Cutlasses and swords are being looked to today. They will probably be reddened within the next week. We are to march light, officers and men. No superfluous baggage, only what you can carry in your haversack, and that is to hold rations as well.

The four 12-pounders and four Maxims were undoubtedly going to have their work cut out to deal with the limitless hordes to be met in the immediate future but the anticipated action did not materialise. By the time the barges containing the Australians and all their bits and pieces had been towed the fifteen miles from the *Salamis's* anchorage to the shore, the threatening concentrations had dispersed — if in fact they ever had existed in the first place.

On the eve of the landing, the flagship, HMS *Barfleur*, gave a concert to which some of the Victorians were invited. One of the guests, Able Seaman Harold Fletcher of the Williamstown Company, wrote home that 'about 30 of us went and we saw heaps of loot, bags of gold watches, gold bars, and rifles of every description'. This was the first time that loot was mentioned by a member of the contingents. It would not be the last.

There may have been no actual threat to life and limb from the Boxers but, at least and last, the Australians were ashore in China. Not

Able Seaman, New South Wales Naval Brigade, North China Field Force, 1900. Drawn by Cathy Wilcox.

however without another alarm and excursion. According to Able Seaman Fletcher again:

There were 300 of us in one barge (on the way to the shore) and we had to stop down in the hold. Most of us had to stand and we were half asleep when the barge bumped into the land. Just then a New South Welshman called out 'For God's sake men come up. The Boxers are on board!' The rush for the deck was something dreadful — we were all falling over each other in our eagerness to get out. Well, the whole thing was a hoax, and as they had taken the ladder away, you can imagine what we suffered. If the men could have found out who it was that had raised the false alarum he would have been killed.

Eventually order was restored and the contingent ashore ready to get into the train which was to take them to their first land-based camp. But as they began to unload their equipment, it was decided that it would be quicker to go to Tientsin by boat.

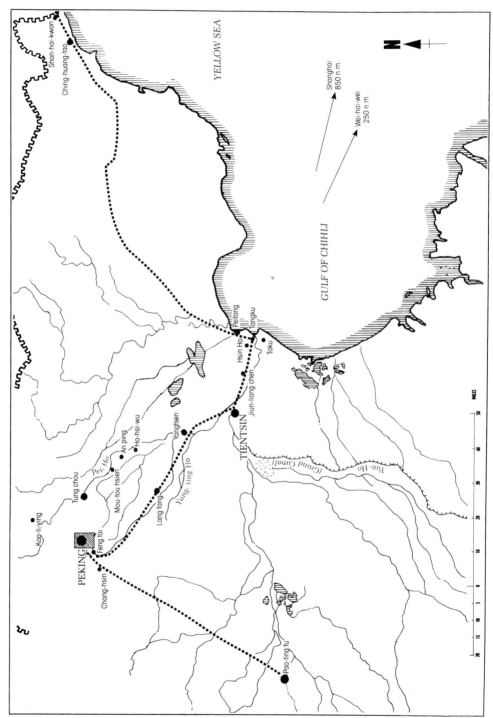

YELLOW SEA

Shan-hai-kwan

Ching-huang-tao

GULF OF CHIHLI

Shanghai
850 n.m.

Wei-hai-wei
250 n.m.

Peitang

Tongku

Toku

Hsin Ho

Jiun-liang chen

TIENTSIN

Kao-li-ying

Tung chou

PEKING

Feng tai

Chang-hsin

An ping

Ho-hsi-wu

Yangtsen

Mou-tou hsien

Long fong

Pei Ho

Yung-ting Ho

Yun-Ho

(Grand Canal)

Pao-ting fu

MILES

Northern China. Broken lines indicates railway system before the uprising.

9

THE PEITANG JOLLY

THE Gulf of Chihli, nowadays called the Bohai Wan, forms the eastern boundary of the North China Plain, which is the delta of the Yellow River. The western part of the gulf is very shallow, as noted in connection with the Allied fleet of warships and transports lying as much as fifteen miles off-shore. The land area in which the Australians operated is very flat. Peking, at the extreme north-west corner of the plain, and lying at the foothills of the Tai Hang mountain range, is probably the highest part of the area, despite an elevation of only 150 feet. The plain is criss-crossed with many, mainly sluggish, rivers and streams, lakes, swamps and marshes. Although the soil is very fertile, the events of the months preceding the Australian's arrival had resulted in it being largely uncultivated. Consequently the wheat, millet and rice fields were overgrown and thick with weeds.

The 1900 population of Chihli Province (which, together with its neighbour Jehol became Hebei Province after 1949 when the municipalities of Beijing and Tianjin were created) is now difficult to estimate but it was possibly in the region of 50 000 000. The provincial capital was at Pao-ting fu, now known as Baoding. All the inhabitants, with the exception of the population of the towns of Peking, Tientsin and Pao-ting fu, were peasants, but their standard of living was high by comparison with the rest of the country. In 1900, however, many had fled, or had been killed, as a result of the tides of war which had

flowed across the area.

A narrow-gauge railway had been built several years before from Shan-hai-kwan through Tangku and Tientsin to Peking. Another was under construction running from Peking to the south-west, where it had reached Pao-ting fu. The progress of this line had been halted by the uprising and it was not repaired for many months. By September the line from Taku through to Tientsin was working under Russian control on a very restricted basis, having first been repaired by gangs of coolies working under Royal Navy supervision. Engines and rolling stock were in a poor condition, most having been destroyed by the Boxers at Fengtai Junction that May. In the interim the preferred method of travel was by sailing junk or sampan along a network of waterways, which included the Grand Canal, running in a north–south direction through the region, crossing and intermingling with the rivers.

By the time the Australians came up the river on their barge under tow of the tug *Heron* the area between Taku, Tientsin and Peking had been thoroughly turned over by several groups of warriors — the Boxers, the Imperial Chinese Army, Admiral Seymour's force, General Gaselee's relief column — and it showed. Assistant Paymaster Wynne, writing for his *Telegraph* readers, found the attitude of the local Chinese worth noting. According to him, they were apparently happy and contented, and struck him as being very little impressed with the destruction and carnage in their midst,

Most of the rolling stock and engines belonging to the railways were destroyed by the Boxers. This is possibly a scene of the engine sheds at Fengtai, south-west of Peking.

and those working on the river poked the floating corpses of their countrymen aside without showing any concern.

The land had been divided into areas for which individual occupying Powers were responsible. The railway from Tientsin to Tangku ran to the east of the river and was the responsibility of the Russians. Here every village was deserted, with every house unroofed and a general air of desolation. Lofts repeats the assertion, in wide circulation at the time, that the Russians either shot their coolies when they had completed their work or herded them into a river to drown. He says he is personally aware that they were driven to work with whips. In contrast, things were returning to what passed for normal on the west bank, which was under the joint control of the Japanese, American and British troops. On this side of the river the houses were now prominently displaying their representation of the flags of one of the occupying Powers, the Japanese flag being predominant probably because of its easy design. The water in the river was, according to Lofts; '... fresh but yellow with mud, whilst on the surface the scum is so thick that it cracks with the waves made by the tug.'

The force anchored for the night some miles short of their destination and was immediately attacked by swarms of mosquitoes and other insects. Able Seaman Bertotto, whose diary describes much of the Victorians' day-to-day activities, called them 'troublesome'. The tug and barge got under way early the next morning and by 1.00 p.m. they arrived off the Tientsin Bund — the main quay area of the town, built up on an embankment. Here they disembarked and marched off to their temporary encampment, the column being headed by the band of the Sikhs at a rather quick pace for the contingent to follow.

After a three-mile march they arrived at their camp at the European racecourse. The camp had already been pitched, even though they still considered themselves to be unexpected, and they spent the afternoon settling in.

That these accommodations had been arranged was partially due to the efforts of Captain P.M. Keogh, a Queenslander, who had tried to join the New South Wales contingent in Australia but, being unsuccessful, had come to China under his own steam and had been welcomed by General Campbell, the British commander at Tientsin, joining his staff as Deputy Assistant Adjutant General, an officer concerned with personnel matters. Their neighbours were the Punjab Infantry, the Bengal Lancers and the Madras Pioneers and all these units did their best to welcome the sailors.

The camp may have come provided with tents, but there was little else in the way of comforts such as furniture or, for that matter, food. Apart from the basic provisions of biscuit, occasional fresh bread and bully beef, they had to provide for themselves and Monday therefore was spent in foraging for vegetables and water, or indeed anything useful. This system of victualling may have been unavoidable but it soon resulted in a policy of the men taking anything they thought they might need. The practice continued until some rudimentary system of local food supply in exchange for money could be arranged.

Swimming in canals such as the one photographed here was inviting sickness.

All hands were sent off to a nearby canal the next morning for a swim '. . . not very enjoyable as the water was very dirty and evil-smelling . . .' This was followed later in the day by their first inspection in northern China, this time by General Campbell. It is hard at this distance to understand the attraction of all these parades and inspections. Whether it was in part due to the fact that few people had seen Australians

before or for some now-forgotten tenet of military discipline is unknown; certainly the accounts of the contingents' activities are studded with references to parades and inspections. A 'make-and-mend' — naval parlance for a half day off duty, originally intended for the making and mending of clothes — was given that afternoon. This was as well, for the next day a messenger arrived in camp with orders to march at once for action against the Chinese-occupied Peitang forts.

Peitang was, and still is, a small coastal village about five or six miles north of Tangku on the north bank of the Pei Ho where it finally debouches into the sea to be surrounded by mud flats, which nowadays have been mainly drained and the area converted into salt pans. The military necessity to occupy the forts which were there arose because the railway line that ran north from Tangku passed near the forts and could be threatened by its guns and troops. The line then ran to the port of Shan-hai-kwan, the only ice-free port in north China and thus of prime importance to the Allies. The forts there had been captured by a small party of Royal Navy bluejackets from the gunboat HMS *Pygmy* under the command of Lieutenant Commander Briggs and Lieutenant John Green in the best RN traditional dashing manner.

Winter was on its way. The high command in Peking decided, none too soon, that a joint force would be required to capture the forts. Detailed for the attack were units from the German, Russian, Austrian and British troops — some 8000 in all. The British contribution of 1500 comprised the Punjab Infantry, the 24th and 34th Madras Pioneers, the recently raised Wei-hai-wei regiment (Chinese troops with British officers), and the Australians. The requirement was for 300 men — 150 from each contingent, the New South Wales half to include their 25 marines. The attraction of fighting, at long last, resulted in many more volunteering to go than were required. They subsequently had ample opportunity to reflect on the traditional fate of those who volunteer.

Things began badly and deteriorated from

there. Firstly they were told to travel light and, being still new to the business of campaigning, did so, even to the extent of not taking any rations. They were to go by train to a position near the forts, but after a rapid march from the racecourse camp through Tientsin city to the station across the river they found that the Russians were only letting the Germans travel on their trains. They had to cross back to the other side of the river and wait for lighters to be procured to take them down the river to get as near to the scene of the anticipated action as possible. A halt of more than four hours ensued while baggage and mules were put on board, and it was midnight when they stepped on board the lighters. The men were put into the hold, where they had to stand up with all the animals, baggage and Sikhs, while the officers stayed on the deck of the lighter. They were rewarded soon after when heavy and continuous rain started to fall.

The lighter was towed slowly down the river, finally grounding on a mudbank well short of their rendezvous position. As it proved impossible to refloat the craft the men had to disembark, form up, and set off to the railway line, where they hoped to meet the others. Captain Gillespie, no doubt as anxious as the rest to get into the promised scrap, set a spanking pace — so much so that by the time they reached the railway line they were exhausted, being out of practice after the long sea voyage from Australia. But, more to the immediate point, they were hungry, not having had anything to eat since the night before — apart from three biscuits and two ounces of tinned meat per man. As they could hear the sounds of battle and see the clouds of black smoke rising ahead, they kept up the gruelling pace. By this time, however, many of the men, the first of them a Sikh, were falling out of the column as the weather was very hot.

Eventually, after a march of eighteen miles and without adequate food, they came upon a Russian field hospital at 6.00 p.m., to find to their fury that the forts had been stormed by the Russians an hour previously. A halt was called

and camp was made for the night, with parties being sent back along the route to collect the stragglers, who included the New South Wales contingent second-in-command, 54-year-old Commander Connor. Needless to say there was no food available and no wood to burn to heat water.

Understandable criticism was levelled at the Russians by the British for going ahead with the assault on the forts without waiting for them. Perhaps they had decided that having, in their eyes, been cheated in the final relief of the capital the previous month they would get their own back. Although the first to enter the city of Peking they had attacked the wrong gate and had got hopelessly behind the troops of the other Powers in the actual relief of the legations. What did emerge, though, was that the Chinese defenders of the forts had slipped away before the attacking force had arrived, leaving only one gun's crew to hold the fort, so at the final charge all the Russians found were four dead Chinese, while their own casualties had been seven killed and thirty wounded.

Part of the peace settlement that the Powers subsequently exacted from the Chinese in 1901 was that the forts at both Taku and Peitang were to be destroyed. In 1984, the remains of both structures still exist. The Taku fort which survived is in the hands of the Chinese Navy, who use it as a small signal station with a staff of two or three sailors. Peitang is deserted, having been largely demolished in 1948 by the Koumintang, but an elderly Chinese man was able to relate how his father had watched the troops attack the fortifications in 1900.

Next morning the force started back to their base, the Australians halting at the station at Jiun-liang Cheng where those who had been most affected by the march of the previous day, 40 in number, caught the train back to Tientsin; the remainder continued on foot to Shin Ho, where they camped for the night and where rations and rum were served at 4.00 p.m., followed by a swim in the river before turning in.

The return march to Tientsin was resumed in

*All that remained of the fort at Peitang in 1984.
The main building was blown up by Chinese
Nationalist troops in 1949; the swampy ground has
been drained and is now partially salt pans.*

*The railway station at Jiun-Liang Cheng in 1984.
Some of the foot-sore members of both contingents
caught the train here to go back to Tientsin after the
abortive attack on the Peitang fort in 1900. It is
now a stop on an important main line track.*

the morning, after the remainder of the rations, by then 'very scanty', according to Able Seaman Bertotto, had been consumed. The water was very bad, 'the worst we have met so far, a thick green scum on top and *smell* very high so that [we] could not drink much of it'. Not surprisingly, after they had got back to their racecourse camp during the late afternoon of 22 September, Bertotto 'got an attack of fever during the night'. He was lucky that it was no worse.

So ended the Peitang forts foray. It had shown that there were many deficiencies in the Australian contingents' preparations for the campaign. However, the lessons learnt could be put to good use in their preparations for the rigours of the next expedition, the planned attack on the Boxer stronghold, Pao-ting fu, provincial capital and reported temporary seat of the Chinese government, who had fled the capital as the Allies arrived.

First though, another inspection, this time by the newly arrived Commander-in-Chief, International Relief Force, Field Marshal Count Alfred von Waldersee. This officer had been sent by the Kaiser to lead the German crusade to avenge the murder of Baron von Ketteler, the German Minister in Peking, whose death immediately before the start of the siege at the hands of a lance-corporal of the Chinese Army had confirmed the Chinese government's complicity in the Boxer movement. As Chester Tan says in his book *The Boxer Catastrophe:*

Field Marshal Count Alfred von Waldersee became the Supreme Commander of the Allied troops in northern China following his arrival at the head of a large contingent of German troops sent by the Kaiser. The photograph shows him at a parade in Peking clad in his Uhlan uniform with the ribbon of the Black Eagle.

The Kaiser said to his men 'just as the Huns one thousand years ago, under the leadership of Attila, gained a reputation by virtue of which they still live in historical tradition, so may the name of Germany become known in such a manner in China'.

The German Army force had arrived, like the Australians, too late for all the glory of the lifting of the siege, and were now casting around for some way to carry out the Kaiser's parting words, which were to the effect that he would not rest until 'German flags floated victoriously over China and, planted on the walls of Peking, dictated the terms of peace'. An expedition to Pao-ting fu seemed a good way to start off.

The Field Marshal's inspection was a drawn out affair. The long-suffering Australians marched three miles to the railway station one day and waited until they were told that he was in fact coming the day after. There was a repeat performance on the second day, and it was not until the third day that the Great Panjandrum arrived, to be greeted by an estimated 400 officers representing the armies of the Allies present, 'all arrayed in full bright uniforms with

This is probably a self-portrait taken by a bearded Lieutenant Spain using the glass-plate negative camera he took to China. He is outside what is probably his tent at the racecourse at Tientsin.

medals in endless profusion on their breasts'. And the by-now footsore Australians.

Meanwhile the routine of the camp had to go on. On 30 September Able Seaman Bertotto was sent out with a party of hands 'to loot a couple of farms and came back with enough vegetables for all hands for a day'.

They also received their first month's pay — 21 Mexican dollars. The Mexican silver dollar was the unit of currency throughout the Far East for many years. The rate of exchange at the time was about ten to the pound sterling.

The first death of an Australian in China occurred during this time. No. 28, Private T.J. Rogers of the New South Wales Marine Light Infantry, died of influenza, and was buried on 6 October. At the time of his death about 25 per cent of the contingent was on the sick list with illnesses such as dysentery, influenza, 'fever' and 'ague' — common complaints whatever the last two may have been in fact. It is not a surprising percentage, considering the conditions in which the contingent were living. Rogers was buried in the churchyard of the English church. It collapsed in the Tangshan earthquake which devastated northern China in 1977 and the site is now a block of apartments.

A hospital had been set up in Gordon Hall, the Tientsin public hall and theatre in the British concession. In 1984 it was being used as sleeping quarters by several Public Security troops who have no idea of the history of their barracks.

Discipline in the contingent had so far been good. However, a problem arose with Able Seaman J. Sylvester, who was charged with talking disrespectfully to officers when he complained about the amount of guard duty he was getting. He was sentenced to 90 days with hard labour in Hong Kong gaol and was returned to Australia soon after serving his sentence as being medically unfit. On his arrival in Melbourne in March 1901 he said he was going to demand a Royal Commission into his case, but nothing seems to have come of it.

On 9 October Connor, somewhat sourly, notes in his diary that the ship's cook was drunk

Gordon Hall, in the British Concession of Tientsin, was converted into a hospital for the British forces in north China in 1900.

A 1984 photograph of Gordon Hall, now used as a barracks by a small detachment of Chinese Security Police. It does not seem to have been greatly altered in the past four or five decades.

all day, and speculates that he must have brought the liquor up from the *Salamis* with him. Connor, as second-in-command of the New South Wales contingent, was responsible for discipline. Thanks to his diary we have a record of the more serious offences and the punishments meted out. Serious offences punished by warrant by Connor are contained in Appendix IV. In almost every case alcohol played a prominent part.

At about this time too the two assistant paymasters Wynne and Wallace are recorded in Connor's diary as having been accused by the French authorities of extortion towards a Chinese washerwoman! No more is known of this tantalising case.

Those who could be spared from guards for supreme commanders or foraging spent their time carrying out daily route marches in preparation for the expedition which lay ahead.

10

A FORCE DIVIDED

THE original plan was that both the Victorian and New South Wales contingents would take part in the expedition against Pao-ting fu, which was about 120 miles south-west from Tientsin. Following what was expected to be the capture and sack of the city, with its population of perhaps 200 000, the New South Wales contingent was to march directly back along the railway line to Peking, roughly 150 miles to the north-east, and take up garrison duties there for the winter. These plans were thrown into last-minute confusion when the New South Wales contingent was ordered to go directly to Peking and not make the detour to Pao-ting fu. This unexpected development upset their arrangements, but with the assistance of the Victorians' transport, they managed to move their gear into Tientsin by 9 October in readiness for the march to the capital the next day. Proceedings had to be halted at one stage to provide a funeral firing party for the burial of a Captain Bruce of the 1st Madras Pioneers, who had died of apoplexy.

The New South Wales contingent's move to Peking was probably a consequence of the Governor of Hong Kong agitating for the return of the Royal Welsh Fusiliers battalion which had been dispatched post haste to take part in the second relief force in July, and whose absence was giving cause for concern by those who thought that further Chinese insurrections would occur. They were the only white British infantry in north China.

Before the New South Wales contingent set off on the 100-mile march to Peking on 10 October, they had been on parade once again, this time to be inspected by Admiral Seymour, who happened to be passing through Tientsin while they were waiting to start on their march, which thus began late, at midday.

The procedure which was followed for the ten-day march was that the men made their way along the tow path by the side of the Pei Ho, while their baggage and other stores, including 30 000 blankets for the garrison in Peking, were carried in junks, towed by teams of Chinese on the river bank and by others who poled their craft along. When there was a suitable breeze, sail was set. The officer in command of this fleet was Lieutenant Staunton Spain, who had brought his unwieldy glass-plate camera with him from Australia. His record of the contingent's time in China takes a prominent place in the illustrations of this book. Midshipman C.E. Murnin, who was also with the junks, kept a diary of his experiences in China with the naval brigade, and his account forms the basis of the following description of the trip from Tientsin to Peking.

The delayed march did not get off to an auspicious start as the contingent followed the Grand Canal instead of the Pei river. This mistake took several hours to become apparent and many more to rectify, so little progress was made on the first day. Things improved from then on, and soon a routine was established, so that the column averaged about ten or twelve miles each day, either along the towpath, in

Admiral Sir Edward Seymour, Commander-in-Chief China Station, and his personal staff. His Flag Captain (Chief of Staff) is Captain John Jellicoe, who later achieved fame at the Battle of Jutland. Also present are his Flag Lieutenant (Commander) and Secretary.

single file, or, when it was more convenient, along the nearby track that connected the two cities. Two days out from Tientsin they came to the town of Yangtsen, where they found a regiment of United States marines who were performing garrison duties there.

This was the first time the Australians had met Americans in the campaign, and they were

The contingent reached the town of Yangtsen two days from Tientsin on their march to Peking. The construction of high flood walls of mud has been carried out since the formation of the People's Republic of China in 1949.

Lieutenant Spain was the officer in charge of the fleet of junks which carried the New South Wales contingent's baggage up the Pei Ho towards Peking in October 1900.

quick to take advantage of the commissary:

> ... a great institution in these parts where stores are few and prices exorbitant. The Australians have discovered the value of cultivating the friendship of the Yankees in this respect, as the privilege has been extended to them of being able to purchase at cost price the little 'extras' and luxuries which help to make life more enjoyable ... the hungry naval men added to their ordinary fare of hard biscuit and tinned meat from the American dry canteens. Salmon, tinned fruit, bacon, tobacco, &c. were obtainable at less than Sydney prices.

These sentiments became familiar to subsequent generations of Australian servicemen. Here also the signal-man for the contingent got 'drunk and stupid'. Knowing the temperance proclivities of the United States authorities it seems unlikely he obtained the wherewithal from their commissary.

By now, two months after the relief of the legations, life was returning to normal in some ways, and the ubiquitous hawkers were doing a roaring trade with eggs at 2½d a dozen, small fowls at 5d each and seasonal fruit, such as

persimmons and pears, at equally low prices. But not all was calm yet. As the contingent made their way towards the capital they came across an agitated Italian soldier who had somehow got separated from his party, and who had been robbed of his rifle.

Four Bengal Lancers who were travelling with the Australians immediately charged off into the high-standing kaoliang, or millet, in pursuit, '... tripped the Celestials with their lances, caught them by their pigtails and brought them back to Captain Gillespie with the rifle'. Their punishment was several hours at hauling the Maxim gun carriages along, after which they were released, much to their surprise and everyone else's. This punishment was extraordinarily light in comparison with that normally meted out to erring Celestials.

In camp one Sunday of the march young Midshipman Murnin felt bored and restless:

> I went through two villages in the afternoon to see if I could get some curios but did not get much. There were a lot of temples and they were full of images, some about 9 feet high and some about 6 inches, but all the places had been ransacked and there was nothing valuable left. I got some pictures off the walls and some Chinese notebooks and envelopes and a

At the town of 'Zunchaw' (Tung-chao) the contingent left the river to march directly to Peking, 10 miles to the west. This 1900 photograph shows the village, now called Tongxian, which is part of the eastern suburbs of the Chinese capital.

Members of the New South Wales contingent shortly after their arrival in Peking, still wearing their sennit hats. They are at the contingent's headquarters at the Chang-wang Palace.

wooden trunk and after having a couple of shots at a dog with my revolver returned to camp.

Eventually they reached the end of their river trip, at the small town of Tung-chao, and after unloading the junks marched the fifteen miles to Peking, being escorted for the last mile by two bands, one from the Sikhs, the other a pipe band from the Baluchistans. Arriving at the British Legation they were divided into three groups and dispatched to take up their accommodations. Three officers and 50 men stayed at the Legation for guard duties, three officers and 60 men were sent to the Llama Temple for similar duties and the remainder set up their headquarters at the Chang-wang Fu palace in the Tartar City. The location of each of these posts is shown on the map below.

Their new quarters provided the first permanent roof for the men since leaving Australia nearly three months before.

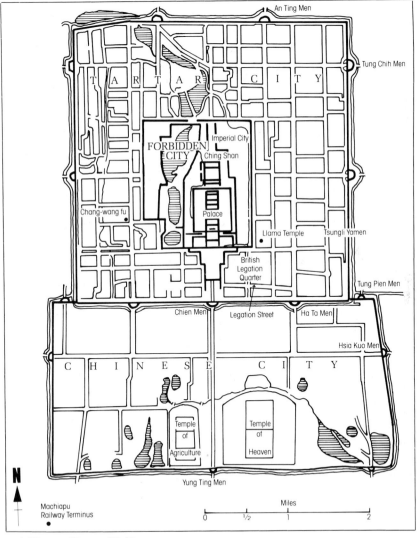

The Tartar and Chinese Cities of Peking

11

THE *PROTECTOR'S* WAR

I N the meantime, the crew of the *Protector* were nearing the end of a period of service during which the men had never left the relative comfort of their ship. Following her arrival in Sydney on 10 August the ship lay off Garden Island to take on coal and essential stores. There, her 'peculiar build' attracted attention from passengers on the passing ferries. After completion of storing which included several stands of Lee-Enfield rifles from the Royal Navy's storehouses, and leave for the crew, *Protector* sailed for Brisbane on Sunday 12 August. She arrived in the Brisbane River on the afternoon of 14 August and was welcomed by a strong contingent of Queensland worthies, led by the Governor, Lord Lamington (whose name is better remembered in another connection). Speeches were made at the naval stores, where refreshments were served.

The terms under which the Admiralty had accepted the cruiser for service, it will be recalled, included the condition that the ship be under the command of a Royal Navy officer, and so in Brisbane command of the *Protector* changed hands. Captain Clare handed over command to Captain Creswell, who had been invalided out of the Royal Navy 22 years previously; apparently this comparatively lengthy break in service was immaterial in guaranteeing his posting as captain of the ship. Clare, as agreed, remained on board as a lieutenant and the ship's navigating officer.

Creswell had long been a proponent of an independent Australian naval force and thus had an intense interest in making the ship as efficient as possible. His views are contained in his memoirs, where he asserts that:

> Imperial defence policy discouraged and depressed any idea of naval development or naval advance in Australia. I had for years striven in every way to overcome this apparently uncompromising objection to Australian naval advance and earnest development of the sea resources available both for Australian defence and for their inclusion in the general scheme of Empire defence. I felt that the *Protector's* success would change this. The fact that a ship commissioned and manned in Australia was efficient for active service and served with and as part of the Imperial navy must overcome all objections.

Creswell took command of the *Protector* on 14 August and the ship sailed from Brisbane the next morning at 6 a.m. At 8 a.m. he read to the crew the Articles of War, a disciplinary code for the Royal Navy, which specifies maritime crimes and their punishments. They were first issued in 1653. (Despite the word 'War' in the title they apply in peace as well as in hostilities.) The ship made her way north inside the Barrier Reef under the charge of a pilot, anchoring every evening and pausing only at Townsville to take on board, as a special service officer, Chief Gunner Blake.

Creswell drove the men hard, with an intense series of exercises and drills in an attempt to bring the ship up to the level of efficiency that he demanded.

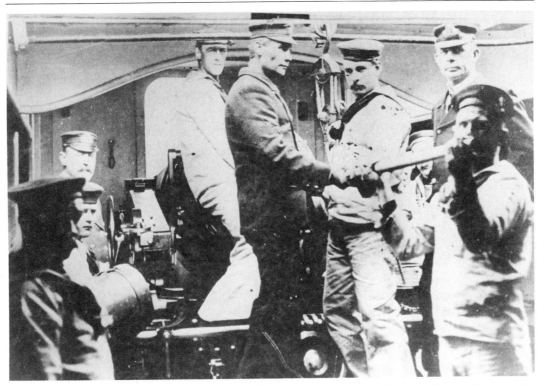

The 8-inch bow-chaser mounted in the bow of the Protector *was one of the largest guns carried in any of Australia's colonial navies. The crew are at drill, and have just rammed the projectile into the breech of the gun. The sailor on the left is carrying the leather container for the cordite propellant charge. The block and tackle are for lifting the 112-pound shell up level with the rear of the breech.*

Some of these exercises were:

* general quarters — where the entire crew muster at action stations
* heavy and light gun drill
* fire stations
* collision mat drill
* abandon ship
* 'bring ship to an anchor and out lower booms' (This was usually practised the evening before entering a harbour.)

A visit to coal the ship and take on board fresh water was made at Thursday Island, the defended coaling station which guarded the Torres Strait at the far north of the Australian continent. While the Burns, Philp contractors loaded the coal, men from the garrison of about 60 from the Queensland Permanent Artillery stationed at the island's Green Hill Fort attempted to supply ten tons of fresh water through a series of makeshift casks, tubs and carts to a long canvas fire hose which carried the precious water along the jetty.

Following replenishment the ship sailed for her next port of call, Ilo Ilo on the island of Panay in the central southern Philippines, on 23 August. The Line was crossed at 4 p.m. on 29 August, with a ceremony much the same as the one on the *Salamis* two weeks before. Able Seaman Jefferys recorded the event in his diary:

There was Father Neptune, his wife, doctor and assistant, barber and boy. The name of each new chum was read out and Neptune's 14 stalwart policemen led him forward. First he was examined by the doctor who gave each man a soft soap pill and handed him over to the barber's boy who smothered him in lather and rolled him onto the stage where the barber finished him off according to how he was liked in the ship. First he worked up and down your face with a large wooden razor, then scrubbed you with a broom, then gave you a sudden push and over you went into the awning (filled with water) where there were four more men ready to duck you till you were exhausted. Then you thought it was your place to assist in ducking the others.

Training continued apace as the ship steamed north through the Banda, Celebes and Sulu Seas on her way to Ilo Ilo. Bombardment of an island was carried out with the ship's main armament without, it is hoped, the expenditure of too many of the precious and irreplaceable rounds of ammunition for the 8- and 6-inch guns, and landing parties, boarding parties and general quarters were continually exercised. The sailors made themselves familiar with the new Lee-Enfield rifles they had obtained from the Royal Navy's stocks in Sydney as well as with the revolvers, cutlasses and boarding pikes brought with them from Adelaide.

According to 'Our Correspondent', writing for the *Herald*, obviously a member of the crew but who has not been identified:

> . . . the port watch were given an hour's lecture on 'First Aid' by Doctor Morris, who is interesting, instructive and amusing at the same time. Imaginary limbs were bound up, arteries and veins stopped from bleeding, until some advanced pupils began to handle bandages and tourniquets as if they wished for a real subject on whom to show their efficiency.

While the sailors honed their military skills, the stokers and engineers down below were keeping the ship moving steadily through the water at ten knots, shovelling coal or greasing bearings in temperatures which rose as high as 124°F. The ship's engines were augmented as often as possible with the sails. When all sail was set, a favourable wind could combine with the engines to give a speed of eleven or more knots.

View from the starboard side of the bridge of the Protector *looking aft with the cruiser under sail. She is carrying a mainsail, main staysail and main top staysail. A canvas windscoop directs air to the engine-room. The very tall funnel is prominent at the right hand side of the photograph. With engine and sail combined* Protector *could make as much as 12 or 13 knots.*

Ilo Ilo was reached on 5 September. Leave was given to the officers only while the ship was being coaled because of the presence of insurgents in the vicinity of the town. The Philippines had ceded to the United States of America in 1898 after the Spanish–American War. However the Filipinos were still conducting a guerilla war against the occupiers and continued to do so until well into 1901.

Protector sailed, fully laden with coal, on 5 September, and ran before a typhoon all the way across the South China Sea. She departed with an estimated twelve hours start on the typhoon. Creswell wrote:

Wind and sea were fairly strong and dead ahead, with a gloomy threatening sky. Clarkson [the engineer] drove and the good little ship bored through it right up to a few hours from Hong Kong. All hatches had to be kept closed. The funnel, the little ship's most commanding feature, radiated heat yards away from it; below the temperature was hot to suffocation; on deck the relief was only too immediate; the half-drowning spray was heavy and continuous.

The ship arrived in Hong Kong on Sunday, 9 September, ahead of the typhoon, which gave little interference to the colony. Creswell notes smugly that the ship caused some consternation by not having any defects and also by being immediately available to continue to the north once she had embarked coal and water. The Commodore-in-Charge, on hearing this, told Creswell that he could have a week in Hong Kong before going north: 'meantime, get anything you want in the way of stores and fittings from the dockyard, and, of course, any work you want done.' This bonanza was very well received by an officer who had spent many years operating under the strictest financial stringency in South Australia. The ship was painted thoroughly and stored to the gunwhales.

At 8 a.m. on 11 September HMCS *Protector* lowered the blue ensign of the colony of South Australia and hoisted the White Ensign of the Royal Navy, becoming HMS *Protector* of the China Station. They then fired a salute of nine guns from the 3-pounder Hotchkiss quick-firers to the Commodore-in-Charge, Hong Kong. The next day the officers all received temporary Imperial commissions, which were followed later by formal commissions on parchment issued by Their Lordships.

Warrant Officer Blake did not get his commission as his name had not been on the list of officers submitted by the South Australian government. This miffed him considerably, as he had to make do with a temporary commission from the Commodore-in-Charge, Hong Kong. Blake's part in the activities of the *Protector* remains a mystery. According to his autobiography, which he published some years

later, he had left the Royal Navy and taken up service on the Chinese Maritime Customs and Chinese Navy for many years. He finally retired and settled in Townsville, where he joined the local detachment of the Queensland Naval Brigade. It is not clear how he came to be included in the *Protector's* crew, where his duties were those of special service officer and interpreter. And he didn't get his £50 outfit allowance, which rankled even more.

The time in Hong Kong was taken up with the crew going ashore to the range on Stone-cutters Island to get some much-needed practice with the rifles they had acquired in Sydney. They also acquired four .45 Maxim machine guns for use in the field if a company had to be landed.

The ship sailed on 19 September for Woosung, where she anchored for the night before crossing the bar and proceeding up the river to Shanghai to refuel. *Protector's* orders were next to proceed to Wei-hai-wei, where she arrived on 30 September, sailing the next day for Taku. En route they had a minor panic and feared they were under attack by a warship which was coming up on them from astern at speed. Eventually it was found to be HMS *Whiting*, one of the destroyers that had taken part in the cutting-out of four Chinese destroyers from their base at Taku in June, when the second relief force had been landed by Rear-Admiral Bruce from the Allied Fleets.

Plans for the immediate future of the *Protector* were meant to have centred around the capture of the fortifications at Shan-hai-kwan, but they were to be disappointed. As has already been mentioned, HMS *Pygmy* did the job alone, with the forts capitulating and the Chinese retreating inland.

Next on the agenda was an attack on the fort at Ching-huang-tao, a few miles down the coast nearer Taku. They arrived off the fort and found HMS *Dido* as well as Admiral Seymour in his dispatch boat HMS *Alacrity*. *Protector* was ordered to land a company, and so 'B' company was paraded fully armed with 150 rounds of ammunition per man. *Dido's* men came on

A technically quite accurate painting of the Protector *in a gale. The small cruiser could well have looked like this as she was battling the typhoon on her way from north China to Hong Kong in the middle of November 1900.*

board and the ship set off round a headland to land the contingent by ship's boats in the next bay. But as the forts came into sight they saw to their anger that the Russians had beaten them to it and were in possession. The attack was cancelled.

The rest of *Protector's* time in China was spent shuttling men and stores between the two ports and carrying dispatches. Able Seaman Jefferys spent two or three days away from the ship in a boat, dragging for and removing submarine mines the Chinese had laid at the approaches to Shan-hai-kwan. He also carried out a survey for the construction of a pier there for the landing of stores in preparation for the Allied Field Force when the railway line to Tangku, Tientsin and finally Peking was re-

paired. Chief Gunner Blake was detached ashore to assist the British General Reid, who was in charge of the stockpiling of these stores, by acting as interpreter for the 400 coolies employed in the task.

By the beginning of November the Admiralty decided they could dispense with *Protector's* services and she was released on 2 November to return to Adelaide. She left north China on 7 November and arrived in Hong Kong on the 15th, having made the voyage in exceptionally rough weather with some damage to the ship's boats and other fittings. The ship's Log carries a report that all holds, magazines and shell rooms were dry, which indicates that the ship's hull, although old, was still in good condition. On arrival in Hong Kong they discovered that the

This view of the forward part of the main deck of the Protector *shows the 8-inch gun at the left of the photograph and the capstan for working the anchor to the right. A rack of rifles is on the starboard side of the ship.*

colony had been hit by an exceptionally late typhoon, causing much damage and driving a Royal Navy gunboat ashore.

Protector went into drydock for a bottom clean — charged to the Royal Navy — where the little dings in the hull were filled with cement and then smoothed off in a small-scale naval panel-beating job. The next few days were spent returning the clothing, weapons and other equipment which had been borrowed from the Imperial authorities. The ship was also replenished with a great deal of canvas gear, for which the Royal Navy probably footed the bill. On Sunday 18 November the ship's company attended church on board HMS *Tamar* and had the rest of the day off.

The ship was decommissioned from the Royal Navy and sailed for Australia on 24 November, calling at Manila in the Philippines and Amboyna (Ambon) on the island of Ceram in the Dutch East Indies (now Indonesia) for coal and water. The next port of call was

Thursday Island for more coal, and after a short stop at Cairns, *Protector*, now HMCS once more, arrived back in Brisbane on 14 December. Here Captain Creswell relinquished command and Captain Clare again became commander of the ship. The Queensland Naval Brigade provided parties of men to clean the ship, a thoughtful gesture which was much appreciated by the South Australians.

Next stop on the journey back to Adelaide was Sydney, which was reached on 18 December. The ship stayed until the New Year, and landed men under the command of Chief Gunner Argent to take part in the celebrations marking the establishment of the Commonwealth of Australia on 1 January 1901. A member of the crew, Petty Officer George Garrison, was the right marker for the whole of the naval line for the review by the first Governor-General, the Earl of Hopetoun.

HMCS *Protector* sailed from Sydney the next day and returned to her home port of Adelaide on Sunday 6 January 1901, having been absent from Australia for five months. During that time she had steamed over 16 000 nautical miles without any material or other defects — a most commendable achievement. Equally impressive was the exceptionally good behaviour of the crew. Their trifling record of punishments is in Appendix IV.

In an interview with Captain Clare the *Adelaide Observer* reported:

What has been the general impression concerning the men?

Throughout I may say the opinion expressed has been complimentary. It is interesting to know that ours was the most healthy ship on the station. While nearly every man-of-war had from 15 to 20 per cent sick, our sick-list was practically nil, with the exception of a few cases of influenza. With regard to the ship, she was certainly the most heavily armed vessel for her size on the China Station. Both Admiral Seymour and Admiral Pearson, who inspected me in Sydney, said she was an efficient ship.

You were disappointed in not going into action?

Yes, we were. The whole ship's crew would have embraced the opportunity had it arisen, but there was not the slightest prospect of it. It has, however, been a great experience. The *Protector* and her crew could take her place anywhere with the British Navy, and it is to the credit of South Australia that she alone of the Australian States was in the position to send a boat like the *Protector* upon active service. You may say that the relations between the officers have been of the most cordial nature. No disputes of any sort have arisen.

Later in the interview: '. . . the ship has not cost a penny in repairs since she left.' Which may have been a true statement then as far as the South Australian government was concerned.

The day after the ship's arrival there was a 'welcome back' social in the Port Adelaide Town Hall and the next day the ship went to Largs Bay to pay off. Each reserve member of the crew was given two weeks pay as a gratuity.

Although this marked the end of the *Protector's* part in the proceedings, the haggling over the amount of money the South Australian government had spent on her deployment went on for a long while after and was still going strong eighteen months later, presumably intensifying when the bills incurred in Hong Kong trickled back to the Admiralty.

12

THE PAO-TING FU JOLLY

BACK in Tientsin the 150 Victorian volunteers were all ready for the start of the expedition which was to take them 100 or so miles inland to the capital of Chihli province, Pao-ting fu. The plan of campaign was for the force, with British General Lorne Campbell in command of the field force in Tientsin but under the immediate command of the French Brigadier-General Bailloud, to make its way across country following the river network which ran in roughly the right direction and would enable them to transport their heavy stores by junk.

In the days before they set out, the Victorians were busy loading their allotted junks with stores, which included the 12-pounder guns brought with them from Hong Kong. At the last minute they were also given the New South Wales contingent's 12-pounders. Together with the Maxims, the force, a total strength of 250 or so, was heavily armed. Their artillery would be of little use if they came under fire while it was still aboard a junk under Chinese control.

Their guns were not the only things the New South Wales men left behind. Able Seaman Bertotto notes in his diary that, after they had departed, nine men of the New South Wales Marine Light Infantry who had been left behind on account of sickness arrived at the camp 'scarcely able to crawl. They were left behind without anyone to attend to them and without food, but we soon fixed them up as well as our resources could admit for we were not very flush with rations.' This is the only report of the

One of the contingent dressed in the uniform of a Manchu official outside a tent in the camp at Tientsin, 1900. The false pigtail is attached to his cap.

85

incident and it is surprising that, if the men were as sick as he reports, they had not been admitted to either the British military hospital at Gordon Hall or the German military hospital in their sector of Tientsin.

After some delay the expedition was ready to start off on Friday 12 October. First however, another parade, this time of all the British elements due to participate. All units were put through a series of manoeuvres, following which they marched past. The Australians took part — naturally — and for the first time paraded their newly acquired transport, which consisted of several commandeered ponies. These ponies, the direct descendants of which still provide much of the motive power in the region, were small, shaggy animals standing under 13 hands. They were better than nothing. In the parade they were used to draw the Australians' Maxim guns and the much-coveted Victorians' transport waggons.

The parade comprised the Australian contingent, the 20th Punjab Infantry, a battery of the Royal Horse Artillery, Bombay Cavalry, Bengal Lancers, 24th Madras Pioneers, 40th Pathans, 1st Sikhs and a pom-pom battery

A Vickers-Maxim 1-inch 1-pounder machine gun, called a pom-pom from the noise it made when firing. Several were captured by the British Army from the Boers in South Africa and pressed into service in north China by the Royal Horse Artillery. The Victorians supplied some of the crews for these guns.

'... truly a column representing troops of the Empire', according to the *Telegraph's* report.

The Vickers-Maxim 1-inch/1-pounder machine guns, called pom-poms from the noise they made, had been captured from the Boers in South Africa and taken into service with the Royal Horse Artillery battery which had been dispatched to north China. The Victorians supplied some of the pom-pom crews.

There was an early start on 12 October. After breakfast at 5.30 a.m. they marched out at 7.00 a.m., leaving Commander Tickell's servant, Boy Gibbs, behind suffering from fever. He subsequently died onboard the hospital ship *Carthage* on his way to the base hospital at Wei-hai-wei and was buried at sea. They met with the rest of the column after about two miles. Six squadrons of Bombay Lancers acted as advance and rear guards. At the head of the column were four squadrons of Bengal Cavalry, then the Royal Horse Artillery with their 15-pounder quick-firing guns and the battery of pom-poms. Next came the Victorians, who were followed in turn by the Madras Pioneers, the Madras Sappers and Miners in their tall cylindrical khaki hats, based on the seventeenth-century shako, and the 31st Madras Light Infantry. In all there were 7500 men in the fighting line and about 1000 camp followers and muleteers.

For modern-day servicemen brought up with Tables of Organisation and Equipment, where every man in a unit has a defined function, the concept of camp followers, except in the sense of battalions of women of easy virtue, may come as a surprise. The Indian Army, drawing as it did on natives of different tribes and castes for its sepoys, had adopted the practice of employing vast numbers of hangers-on to carry out the multifarious tasks that the rank and file for one reason or another either would not, or could not, carry out. Each unit of the Indian Army travelled with an attendant horde of dhobi-wallahs to do the laundry, syces (grooms) for their horses, sweepers, artisans of all descriptions, muleteers, officers' cooks and servants, amounting to an enormous train, all to be fed

Thursday   October 11th   0 0

Inspection by General Lorne Campbell at 10:30 am
remainder of day packing & storing gear not required on
the march, orders to march out at 7:30 tomorrow morning

Friday   October 12th   0 0

Turn out at 5:30 am had breakfast; Boy Jibbs taken
to Base Hospital, suffering from fever 6:30 am
Marched out at 7:0 am. met coloumn about two
miles outside Tien-Tsin consisting of one battery of
R.H.A. with 15 lbs, one battery of Pom Poms. Madras
Pioneers, Madras Sappers & Miners, 31st Madras
Light Infantry; four squadrons of Bengal Cavalary,
six squadrons of Bombay Lancers, making in all
about 7.500 men in the fighting line; and
about 1.000 camp followers and mulateers,
Formed up with Artillery and Cavalary leading
followed by the W.N.C; and Indian Troops. and
Bombay Lances, as advance and rear guards,
Marched off at 9:30 am. Halt for ten minutes at

A page from the diary of William Bertotto, in China with the Victorian contingent. In this extract he details the force that left Tientsin for the expedition to Pao-ting fu.

and cared for in a rudimentary way. It made soldiering more comfortable.

The march from Tientsin to Pao-ting fu took ten days, a day's march averaging ten or so

'This is a very old city, the walls of being near circular . . . In some places large trees apparently a hundred years old were growing out of them.' From the description of the village of Rou-tiu in Able Seaman Bertotto's diary.

miles. According to Able Seaman Bertotto, two days out his unit came across a cow, which they killed, thus having fresh beef for supper. They also went down to the river and met the supply junks from whom they obtained bread and their tents, so they had a 'good meal and turned in early'. By this time the weather, which had remained hot for an unseasonably long time, had changed and was turning cold and wet. This made the going difficult, with the result that the contingent only managed a few miles the next day, when they arrived at the town of Wo-yang hu, which attracted the attention of some members on the lookout for food. They had 'a fair amount of success in fowl, eggs and maize meal, so that when we returned to camp we made a good meal of eggs and poultry and cakes which we made from the maize meal; the best meal since landing in China'.

On the march again the next day they arrived at Rou-tiu:

This is a very old city, the walls of it being near

circular and judging from the state of them must of been built about the time that the 'Ark' stranded. In some places large trees apparently a hundred years old were growing out of them and it is not likely that they were allowed to take root while the walls were new. Here in a temple which stood between the walls and the city, (which are about a mile apart) ten 'Boxers' were captured with two field guns and a quantity of ammunition, by the R.H.A.

While foraging about in the city in the hope of picking up something for supper we came into a large house, to all appearances a bank, where we found ten or twelve large stone jars each four feet high by two feet wide filled with brass and copper cash. We emptied some of them hoping to find some silver coin, but we were disappointed. The large quantity of cash was no use to us so we left it behind us.

Next thing we found was a fair-sized room more than half-full of boxes of gold leaf, but these being too bulky to carry we had to leave them also. We found some maize meal and

Beheading was the normal method employed to execute Boxer prisoners. The photograph shows a Japanese Army execution. Loyal Chinese Army soldiers look on.

millet and three fowls so we returned to camp and made a meal off them and turned in. The prisoners were shot at sunset.

By 20 October rations were getting very low, and all they had to eat that day were two 'jupatees, (cakes made of Indian corn flour and baked on ashes) per man'. However things started to look better when they arrived at Shih-pha chow that afternoon. They occupied the village, ten men to a house, and soon had fires going to keep out the cold and damp:

There being plenty of fowls and eggs in the house which my tentmates and I had taken for the night we had a good supper, after which we cooked sufficient for us for tomorrow. Meanwhile the native owner of the house, having first moved his family to some place of safety, busied himself in getting firewood for us and getting children's clothes stowed away in case

we should take a fancy to them, but I for one preferred his poultry and eggs. And before we turned in we gave him a good meal and then he went to sleep on the roof, the rain having ceased he slept till we called him at daylight next morning.

They reached Pao-ting fu the next day and were spared the trouble of laying siege to it because the officials surrendered the city.

While the Victorians were helping to restore some order in the city they released a party of missionaries — amongst whom was the Green family, who had experienced 'terrible hardships during their confinement'. The retribution-obsessed Germans however set off for the hills to the south to attack a reported Boxer stronghold. They soon found they had bitten off more than they could chew, and the Bombay Lancers and the pom-pom battery had to be sent to their rescue. The Green family were sent back to Tientsin with an escort of Victorians under Warrant Officer Marwood.

The remaining Victorians were placed on guard over a number of prisoners found guilty of the massacre of missionaries and traders. They handed them over to the Germans to be shot: 'so they were taken outside the walls, made to dig their own graves and then stood in line and shot, they were rolled in and covered within an hour of their being handed over.' The next day their prisoners were the Mandarins of the city, and the Victorians spent an uncomfortable night wondering if their sympathisers in the more than half a million population would try to rescue them, but this did not eventuate and they were handed over for execution to some French Zouaves who had come with the column from Tientsin.

These events were minor compared to the executions of the Provincial Treasurer, the military governor of the Province and the colonel commanding the Chinese cavalry, who had jointly surrendered Pao-ting fu to the Allied Powers on their approach. According to a contemporary report which appeared in the *Herald*:

It was a Bland Holt [Joseph Thomas 'Bland' Holt (1853–1942) was a contemporary Australian entrepreneur noted for his spectacular stage productions] kind of execution, staged on a scale of magnificence never before attempted on active service. The French and Germans stage-managed the whole affair and it was certainly impressive.

A large open space, empty but for the guards stationed at each entrance and at each platform in the centre. A bugle blast, a roll of drums, the even tread of marching men, and 3000 troops file in, and place themselves around. Another flare of bugles and roll of drums — enter the victims and the executioners. The chief bows low to the victims, then to the audience, in the manner of an acrobat about to perform a difficult feat. The assistants do likewise, and throw themselves into statuesque postures.

Another signal, and the first victim was forced on his knees, two assistants held him

firmly by the shoulders, a third seized his pig-tail, a fourth handed his axe to the executioner, and he balanced it carefully, raised it slowly to the height of his shoulder, lowered it till the edge touched the bare neck, and left a scarlet mark. Once, twice, and he swung it with all his might. There was a spurt of blood, a few convulsive movements, the man with the pigtail tugged savagely, the threads of hair parted and it was all over . . .

By now it was obvious to even the bloodthirsty Germans that the strength of Boxers in the area was insignificant, and so the force set out on the return march to Tientsin. The route was much the same as that taken on their outward march, but this time they concentrated on a 'scorched earth' policy, ransacking, looting and finally blowing up and setting fire to almost every village and small town. There is no contemporary explanation for this behaviour in any account of the expedition.

A stop was made at Mou-tou shien on 30 October, where, Bertotto notes, 'the officers looted this city'. The next day in the village of Li-kung-pao the contingent caught 'six Chinese trying to steal some of the mules (which we commandeered here on our last visit), brought them in at 6.00 p.m. and they were shot at 6.30'; which seems a harsh punishment to men who, after all, had been the beasts' original owners.

Well on the way back to Tientsin they next came upon the town of Wen-an where there were supposed to be Boxers and the city hostile. Bertotto's diary records:

The Madras Sappers and Miners were sent to lay mines under the Main (North) gate and the North East and North West corners of the Wall, over each of which stood a large watch-tower over a hundred feet high and as artillery was useless on such a massive structure the mines were to be for the morning if a peaceable entry was still refused . . .

. . . the mines laid yesterday were fired at 7.45 a.m. with the result that the Main Gate and both corners of the Walls with the watch towers, were in a heap of ruins by 8.00 a.m.

The west arsenal in Tientsin in 1900 with a moat in the foreground.

and as a great crowd of the inhabitants had assembled at these places and all along the Walls evidentaly preparing to open fire the blowing up shook them up a little and shook some of them out of this world altogether.

We marched away from Wen-an at 9.00 a.m. leaving the Artillery and Cavalry to square up accounts with the wounded and prisoners, and as heavy firing was heard until late in the afternoon I reckon they did it all right. We burnt and looted two villages between 10.00 a.m. and 12.00 a.m.

This activity formed the pattern of the remainder of the expedition.

The next incident occurred two days before they arrived back in Tientsin, when at about 6.00 p.m. some war junks which had been captured by the river column had had their explosives unloaded and placed on the river bank ready to be destroyed. They suddenly blew up, killing over 60 Indians and Chinese coolies and injuring many more; several people died before reaching hospital in Tientsin.

The Victorians arrived back in Tientsin at noon on 7 November, having been in the field for 25 days. During that time they had marched over 200 miles and taken part in innumerable sackings, looting, arson, pillage and executions without coming into contact with the enemy, let alone coming under his fire.

Able Seaman Bertotto looked at things from the point of view of the footslogger called on to do all the work and thus his description falls somewhat short of the more formal official accounts of the expedition. Apart from the general bloodthirstiness of the Germans, the reason that Pao-ting fu had been selected as the target of the drive was that a number of French and other nations' missionaries and their families had been under siege there since June and it was thought necessary to find out what had happened to them. While they were about it, they could try to make contact with the main Boxer force, believed to be in the area with headquarters in the city itself, and bring them to battle. The plan was for the Peking column of 3500 British, French and German troops to leave the Chinese capital at the same time as the numerically stronger column from Tientsin and for both forces to arrive simultaneously for a joint attack.

The whole plan was rendered useless by the activities of a French 'flying column' which had left Peking surreptitiously and which occupied Pao-ting fu four days before the main body turned up. The Indians and Australians in the Tientsin column would have rendezvoused late as they had been forced to make a long and difficult detour round a lake not shown on their maps, arriving two days after the remainder of General Bailloud's force. Both incidents created some ill-feeling amongst the troops of the nations in the expedition, an ill-feeling that was to intensify in the months that lay ahead.

Winter was now rapidly approaching. Fortunately, in their absence, the authorities had done something about the Victorians' accommodation. On their return to Tientsin they moved directly from their tents at the racecourse into a large godown (a word used widely in Asia to describe a large storehouse). This was their barracks and headquarters until they left China five months later.

13

SETTLING IN: PEKING

WHILE the Victorians had been on the rampage, the New South Wales contingent had been assuming the tasks that, with few exceptions, they would carry out until their departure for Australia. This essentially static role was not one shared by their companions in the International China Field Force. By the end of the summer of 1900 most of the units which had arrived from Europe had been given an opportunity to distinguish themselves during expeditions against various areas thought to be Boxer strongholds. Apart from playing a leading role in the Pao-ting fu expedition, the Germans had conducted 'search and destroy' forays into the plains of northern China. The Italians, who had a detachment of their Bersaglierie in the field, and the French, had been busy too.

There was widespread condemnation of the behaviour of the Russian troops, whose brutality soon became legendary, and the United States was on the point of withdrawing its forces altogether, mainly because they were desperately needed to assist in the subjugation of the Philippines.

Sending the New South Wales contingent into the field as part of these expeditions does not appear to have been considered, either by the contingent or by the high command. Perhaps this was because they were regarded as long-term residents of Peking; certainly they weren't going to be withdrawn for some time to come. So they settled into their quarters and started to make them as comfortable as possible.

After the occupation of Peking by the International Force in mid-August the city had been divided into geographic areas in which the policing and civil administration, in the absence of the Chinese authorities, were made the responsibility of one of the Powers. The initial duties of the contingent were described in a dispatch to the *Sydney Morning Herald* dated ten days after their arrival in Peking:

The detachment based at the British legation under the command of Lieutenant Roberts provides guards for the entrances to the legation, the Hong Kong and Shanghai Bank, orderlies for the British headquarters and also fires the noonday gun.

At the Llama temple in the Imperial City, Lieutenant Hixson's company furnishes guards over the temple, at a godown in which much loot was stored and also the big hole in the city wall made by the Boxers during the siege and through which it was expected that any further attack would be made.

The Headquarters company at the Changwang Palace supply guards for the main entrance and 20 men, including four marines, are engaged on police duties in the Tartar City.

In a philosophic section of his dispatch, Assistant Paymaster Wallace goes on to say:

... the New South Wales contingent are greatly disappointed in their bad fortune. [At not going on the Pao-ting fu expedition.] Their only consolation is that they came prepared for any contingencies that might arise, and if they

The International China Field Force comprised soldiers, sailors and marines from the following countries: (l. to r.) Great Britain (RHA), United States (Marine Corps), Australia (Naval Contingent), Great Britain (Indian Army), Germany, France (Zouaves), Austrian Empire, Italy (Bersaglierie) and Japan.

have to return without firing a shot it will simply be because the opportunity of showing their fighting qualities, with the corresponding chances of distinguishing themselves, has not been afforded.

In the matter of furnishing their accommodation, Connor notes in his diary that:

> The 1st Sikhs found a Boxer's house near us and taking all they wanted they kindly sent us word that we might come over and take any odds and ends left. The Mess thereby benefited considerably but very little individually.

Soon after their arrival they had their first 'excitement', to use Wallace's term. The detachment at the Llama Temple had been busy one evening when a fire was discovered in a house which lay between their headquarters and the store of silk they were meant to guard. They extinguished the fire without too much difficulty by pulling down the walls of the house thus smothering the blaze:

> A Chinaman was caught red-handed in the act of committing arson and was arrested after a smart chase. Evidence was given showing him to be a notorious Boxer, and, according to our interpreter, the house he had set on fire was his own. He had sent his wife and family away,

and his idea was that if the conflagration spread it might reach the silk godown on the one hand or the temple on the other.

'Tie his hands and feet,' said Lieutenant Hixson (the officer in charge of the detachment

The main entrance to the British Legation in Peking after the siege had been lifted, taken from across the canal. The defenders had constructed fortifications around the gate, which they named Fort Halliday.

A Company, New South Wales contingent pose with their 12-pounder quick-firing naval field gun in Peking.

at the Llama Temple), 'and put him in the guard room. We will shoot him in the morning.'

This was their first execution. They had had floggings, plenty of them, but this was their first life. There was a formal report to General Gaselee, and back came the death warrant.

Five minutes later it was endorsed. Blind-folded, with his hands tied behind him, the prisoner was led out and stood by the ruined wall of the house he had set fire to.

Five men formed the firing party.

'Fire where the paper is pinned,' said Sub-Lieutenant Black, the officer in charge. 'Ready, aim, fire!'

The Residence of the British Minister at the Legation in Peking after the relief. The building had occupied a key position in the 55-day siege.

Part of the New South Wales contingent's headquarters at the Chang-wang Palace in Peking. There is a light covering of snow on the roofs. The palace was immediately outside the Forbidden City to the south-west. See map on page 77.

Midshipman Bracegirdle decked out in summer field uniform, which he had no opportunity to wear in action in China.

It was, at six paces, not a difficult target for the sharpshooters of the New South Wales Naval Brigade. And so, either to deliver the signal or the coup de grace, the sword given to Bertie Black by his colleagues at Messrs G.S. Yuill did come in handy after all.

The New South Wales contingent was also suffering loss of life. An able seaman, J. Hamilton, died in hospital at Tung-chao on 6 November, having been left there by the contingent on their way to Peking from Tientsin. The cause of death was given as exhaustion following dysentery. He had been a sailmaker by trade, and had continued this occupation in the brigade. He was buried in a soldier's grave on the banks of the river, uncoffined and wrapped in a flag. Next to die was their doctor, Staff-Surgeon John Steel, who was discovered dead in his room late in the evening of 10 November. According to evidence produced at the inquiry into his death he had not been well for some time and had been in the habit of taking a dose of chloral hydrate as a sleeping draught. On the night in question it was assumed he had taken an overdose by mistake.

Connor, on the other hand, takes a much less charitable view. In his diary he makes frequent references to Steel's behaviour but he stops short of actually indentifying the cause:

22 Oct. Steel very bad indeed. Captain (Gillespie) noticed it.

23 Oct. Steel got shopped this morning. I wonder if it will have an effect. He was mooching around after the men at grog time.

9 Nov. (The day before he died) The Captain showed me a draft letter re Steel but as the Dr was in bed I could not get at him.

His funeral was a somewhat grander affair than sailmaker Hamilton's, for he was buried with full military honours in the temporary graveyard in the grounds of the British Legation.

His body, together with those of other casualties of the siege, was later exhumed and re-interred in the British cemetery, about a mile north of the great British gate, which places it somewhere near the rear of the present Beijing

The New South Wales Ambulance Section at their headquarters at the Chang-wang Palace in Peking. Staff-Surgeon Steel is at the right of the photograph. The section named their quarters 'Katoomba Cottage'.

Hotel. A November 1984 search for this cemetery was abortive, due to the destruction of all records at the British Embassy in Peking by the Red Guards in 1968. The present British cemetery in Peking is elsewhere and is said not to hold any bodies from the previous graveyard.

The cortege was led by a contingent of 100 bluejackets and marines, followed by a detachment of artillery and the pipers of the 1st Sikhs. The coffin was borne on a gun carriage and on each side walked the principal mourners, including Captain Gillespie and Commander Connor. Lieutenant-General Gaselee and his staff and Brigadier-General Sir N. Stewart, his chief of staff, also attended. 'Their presence was greatly appreciated by the sorrowing contingent,' said the *Herald*.

A medical inspection was held by the British army surgeons to weed out any men who might not be capable of withstanding the rapidly approaching severe winter weather. Three men, Able Seamen Vine, Conwell and Oliver, were considered to be unsuitable and were dispatched to Tientsin en route for Australia, eventually arriving in Sydney on board the SS *Changsha*.

On 21 November the final boat convoy for the year left Peking for Tientsin. For the preceding fortnight the temperature had hardly risen above freezing and already there was ice on the river and in the shallow waters of the Gulf of Chihli. The contingent had food, fuel and warm clothing and were in a good state to face the oncoming winter. Having thus cleared the decks, the men settled down to their routine.

14

SETTLING IN: TIENTSIN

BACK in Tientsin the Victorians were of course experiencing similar living and climatic conditions. One task fell to Able Seaman Bertotto while the weather still permitted.

Wednesday November 14th

All .303 ammunition called in: J. Young L.S. (Leading Seaman) and myself received orders at 11.00 a.m. to proceed up the river Pei Ho to escort a number of Chinese Christians to Tien Tsin. So we got ready, taking 300 rounds of ammunition each and two days rations and at 11.30 a.m. we left our quarters accompanied by a native guide, and an interpeter. After leaving we met two Japanese Cavalarymen, who were also to accompany us, so we took 'rickshaws and rode to the outside of the City, and down to the river above the locks where we engaged two snake boats, of course looking out for the fastest sailers that we could get and got our gear onboard and started up the river at 2.15 p.m. There was a strong breeze blowing and so we made good headway; we reckoned that we done a good eleven miles an hour. Arrived at a villiage at 4.30 p.m., and as the wind hauled ahead we took up lodgings for the night — had a good supper and turned in, with our side arms on and our rifles loaded alongside of us, quite a happy family, two Australians two Japanese and two Chinese all in one room and slept with on eye open, but nothing of note occoured during the night which was terribly cold.

Thursday November 15th

Turned out at 5.30 a.m., had breakfast and got ready for a start but when we got down to the river we found that our two snake boats which we left in charge of four Chinese boatmen moored to the bank were both firmly frozen in; but seeing some other boats in mid-stream we arranged with two of them so as to continue the journey, then we paid off the other two and started up at 8.30 a.m. Arrived at Kwang-Su Canal at 10.00 a.m. Going up here we had a head wind for about a mile and so we were compelled to tow the boats, the Canal being frozen to about one inch thick over the whole surface made towing hard work, while walking along the banks towing we were passing over heaps of human bones all along the Canal, evidentally dumb witnesses of some fierce battle, or perhaps of a plague. About 11.00 a.m. we came to a bend in the Canal, which brought the wind on our beam, so we got aboard again and set sail, the wind being strong we made very good progress, considering we were forcing our way through ice as well as water, nevertheless, by carrying as much sail as possible we got a good ten miles an hour out of the boats. Arrived at the head of the Canal and secured two (panchaus) native carts and two good teams of ponies and started for Wong-Chang across country at 1.30 p.m., learning now for the first time since leaving Tien-Tsin where we were bound to. The ponies proved to be good goers, passed through Pei-Chang at 4.30 p.m. Arrived

Able Seaman William Bertotto flanked by two of his mates (unidentified) from the Victorian Naval Brigade in the winter uniforms which had been supplied by the Canadian government. Note the clay pipes he and one of his mates are carrying.

at Wong-Chang at 6.00 p.m. it being then quite dark but our guide soon found the people that we wanted who were almost wild with delight when they knew that we were to escourt them out of the City, which was in a state of seige. They brought us food of all descriptions, enough for a score of men, and we being hungry had a good meal, after which we made all necessary arrangements to have everything ready for an early start as it would be unsafe to attempt to leave the City after daylight, for our Interpter told us that the 'Boxers' outside the City were over 20 000 strong. We put up for the night in the house of one of the Christians they preferring to keep guard, which suited us as we were tired so we turned in and slept till 4.00 a.m.

Friday November 16th

Turned out at 4.30 a.m. and had breakfast, then we got our waggons and carts all ready with 55 women and children 4 merchants and 2 of the City officials, we made a start at 5.30 a.m. we made all possible speed till sunrise, and by that time Wong-Chang was nearly out of sight behind us we had come thus far without being seen so we eased our speed so as not to be too hard on the animals as their strength might be required later on. Passed through Pei-Chang at 10.00 a.m. here we met a British outpost consisting of 25 men and 2 officers of the 31st Madras Light Infantry, who reported to us that there were no rebels to be found in this City, so we were able to choose our pace. Arrived at the head of the Kwang-Su Canal about noon where we found our two boats waiting. But we had to secure two more boats to carry all our pilgrims with all their traps so it took us till 2.00 p.m. before we had them all ready for a start down. We left the villiage at the head of the canal at 2.15 p.m. We were not too soon getting away from here as the ice was getting very thick there

only being a channel barely wide enough for the boats to pass through which had been kept open by our two boats continually passing up and down for that purpose. Entered the Pei Ho at 3.30 p.m. which being clear of ice we were able to make good headway. Anchored in midstream at dusk (5.30 p.m.).

Saturday November 17th

Turned out at 4.00 a.m. and continued down the River till 6.30 a.m. when we arrived at a lock and finding that the lock could not be opened before noon. So we transhipped all the gear and pilgrims into two large junks which were lying below the lock continued down the River at 10.00 a.m. Arrived in Tien-Tsin at 1.15 p.m. and landed all the pilgrims and quartered them in a compound in charge their friends, after which they made us some presents and then we left them and returned to our own quarters.

A welcome improvement was the issue, a few days later, of the first set of winter clothing. They had left Australia with blue serge uniforms and greatcoats, but these were quite inadequate for the severe winter which was fast approaching. The British had obtained some winter clothing from the Canadian government and this was to prove invaluable. Two hundred and sixteen blankets, 2nd quality, had been purchased at cost of 3s a pound and the total weight of 860lb cost the Victorian taxpayer £129. One extra blanket was issued to each of the men of the Victorian contingent presumably to augment the one he had brought with him from Australia and which by then must have been getting pretty threadbare.

With final issue of 'Balaclava' caps and six yards of 'karkee' serge at the beginning of December, all was ready for the first heavy snow of the winter, which fell on 6 December.

15

STAYING ON

Now that the season — and the necessity — for punitive expeditions against the Boxer seemed to be over, pressing requirements elsewhere forced the British government to re-deploy their forces. So there was a general redisposition, and the commissary staff in China were told not to order more supplies for the Indian Army troops, thus giving a clear indication that they would soon be returning to their home country.

The matter of the Australians and the length of time that the Imperial government could reasonably be expected to retain their services was discussed in London. As a result, both Premiers of New South Wales and Victoria received telegrams from Mr Chamberlain in the middle of November. The messages said that the naval commander-in-chief, to whom they had originally been seconded, stated that it was absolutely necessary to retain the Australian naval contingents and that the military disposition of troops had been made under the belief that they would remain for the winter. They were, the telegrams went on, most useful and eminently suited for police work in China and in guarding the legation. Could they please be allowed to stay?

The message caused some bewilderment in Sydney as the length of service had not been raised before and the intention was that the men be given for service to the Imperial government for any reasonable length of time for which they might be required. In his reply Sir William Lyne said that the contingent could remain until February or March. His Victorian colleague replied that he had pleasure in complying with Mr Chamberlain's request.

Neither politician apparently saw the request as an example of prudent yard-arm clearing by London in view of the different status the naval brigades would have following Federation of the Australian colonies only six weeks off. Nor, as far as can be ascertained, did they seek the opinions of their respective field commanders, Captain Gillespie and Commander Tickell.

Now that the niceties had been observed, all was clear for both contingents to organise themselves for the winter. The New South Wales contingent of 254 had settled in to their quarters by the middle of November. Of this number 96, including the Marine Light Infantry detachment, were at contingent headquarters at Chang-wang fu in the Tartar city; 64 men were occupying the Llama temple and another 63 were at the Legation. Twenty men were on police duty in the capital and of the balance seven were either still in hospital in Tientsin or on their way back to Peking to resume full duty; two men were in the British hospital at Wei-hai-wei convalescing. Two men were on permanent detachment to the Tientsin garrison — acting Warrant Officer Corbin, as assistant transport officer and acting Warrant Officer Hinnem, as a superintendent of police.

A routine was soon established. In a newsy letter published in the *Herald*, one of the marines describes his activities:

So here we are at last, quartered in rooms at

Indian Army guard, Peking 1900. By the beginning of 1901, the British were planning on withdrawing the majority of their Indian Army troops from north China and so the Australian colonial governments were asked if their contingents could stay in China until the northern spring.

the palace and likely to spend about six months here, as it is winter here.

This morning (5 November) the water in the chatties — bowls about 4 ft. in diameter — was frozen into ice ¾ inch thick ... We have been here 12 days and I have done two guards already and attended the funeral of a Royal Welsh Fusilier. I and five other marines had to carry the coffin. Being on guard here is rather lonely work. Firing going on all night, wild dogs snarling and fighting all around, trees groaning, a wild cat running between one's feet, and a piercing cold wind ... The wild dogs have eaten all the dead Chinese in the streets, thousands of them [sic], and they are starving. They are as bad as wolves. We buy plenty of eggs and fruit, and can buy cocoa, tinned butter, condensed milk, sugar &c. from the Commissary. I was escort at a court martial yesterday.

... We are supplied with bread, jam, meat, vegetables, rum, tea, and sugar ... As I write there are about one hundred dromedaries un-loading coal outside.

... We were paid on the 1st — 23 dollars 25 cents. I spent £1 12s 6d on tucker yesterday. Talking of the cold, some of the rooms have bought stoves and keep them going all night. Two of the four walls in our room are entirely glass, and one wall of the next room, being glass, fell out this morning with a crash, partly on the slumbering occupants. We went to church in Prince Ching's Theatre yesterday with the 12th Battery. We trade in dollars, cents, or cash; ten dollars to the £, 100 cents to the dollar, and 5 cash to a cent. That is 15 cash to a penny, and you get a meal for 5 cash. They sell papers, grapes, persimmons, peanuts, apples, tripe and Chinese dishes down the markets. We do guard from tatoo to reveille with five or six rounds in the magazine, and one in the chamber and a fixed bayonet. We rise at 6.30, roll call at 7, breakfast at 7.45, fall in at 9, dinner at 12.30, leave from 2 to 5.30, tea at 4.15, first post at 8.30, second at 9, lights out at 9.15 p.m.

(The practice of using Chinese stoves, which burn coal and which give off a great amount of carbon monoxide, in airtight rooms was to have

Some of the detachment of New South Wales Marine Light Infantry at their headquarters in the Chang-wang palace in Peking shortly after their arrival in 1900.

tragic consequences later, when one morning a German officer was found dead in his room, having been asphyxiated by the fumes from his stove.)

Each company of the contingent had a portion of the city's British sector to administer. The Australians soon set up a form of municipal government to supervise the cleaning and lighting of the streets in their sector. They also carried out normal police functions and the officers were appointed magistrates with jurisdiction over the Chinese.

One case involved two Chinese. One, a Christian, contended that the other, who was a servant of the prominent Chinese statesman Li Hung Chang and who was relying on the protection of his exalted master, had attempted to swindle him. For the defence it was alleged that the Christian had endeavoured to extort money from the heathen by threatening to use foreign influence against him.

According to Assistant Paymaster Wynne in a dispatch to the *Telegraph:*

> Both parties lied considerably, and we ended up matters by flogging the heathen, to show him the extent to which Li Hung Chang could protect him, and by flogging the Christian for using his alleged Christianity for motives of immediate personal profit, instead of to prepare himself for the hereafter, as all good Christians should. Rugged justice, perhaps, but we have no laws here that require a university education, and life-long study for their correct administration. We just deal out plain, unadulterated justice, and it gives satisfaction, if not pleasure, to all.

Now well into his pontifical stride, Wynne continues:

A member of the New South Wales Marine Light Infantry detachment in his winter uniform supplied by the Canadian government.

A flogging is not such a bad thing when you are used to it. The offender is tied up to an altar in the court yard and thrashed with a locally manufactured cat. He squeals a good deal during the process, re-adjusts his nether garments when it is over, kneels down and touches the ground three times with his forehead in acknowledgement of our great mercy. He usually expects to be executed and goes away as if nothing extraordinary had happened.

On execution by firing squad, he writes:

When the number to be despatched is large, each prisoner is attended to by three men, and at a given signal they fire a volley. Should the victim stir after that a dexterously-handled bayonet or a revolver shot hurries his exit. We are growing callous — that is part of the Eastern education. Until you can bring yourself to regard the Chinaman as something less than human, considerably less, you are at a disadvantage.

And:

The future of the Chinese is a fearful problem. Look on the frightful sights one sees on the streets of Pekin, the pock-marked, the deformed, the blind, the hideous yellow faces, with their rows of blackened broken teeth, the sickening blood-red eye sockets, telling of horrible disease. See the filthy tattered rags they wrap around them. Smell them as they pass. Hear of their nameless immorality. Witness their shameless indecency, and picture them among your own people — ugh! it makes you shudder.

Fortunately for the readers of the *Telegraph*, and posterity, Wynne's reporting normally wasn't quite this bad. Assistant Paymaster Wallace usually played for safer ground, preferring straightforward reporting to the topics that attracted his colleague's professional attention:

At the race meeting which was held on Saturday afternoon [17 November] last there was a large attendance of the Allies' officers, including Count von Waldersee, the German Field-Marshal, and his large staff, Lieutenant General Sir A. Gaselee and his staff, and General Richardson, the American General besides

Assistant Paymaster Wynne appears on the far left of the men seated in this 1901 photograph taken in Peking. Sitting in the row are also Lieutenant Hixson, Sub-Lieutenant Creer and Midshipman Bracegirdle. Wynne wears a comparatively casual form of dress, perhaps in keeping with his alternative status as a newspaper correspondent.

other notabilities in the diplomatic world. The German officers in their handsome grey top-coats and clanking swords were in the majority. An Indian pipers' band and an American brass band discoursed music on the lawn. The race for Chinese and Manila ponies, over half a mile, was the great attraction, and 27 officers from the different armies lined up at the start. New South Wales was represented by Sub-Lieutenant Y.G. Lindeman on Captain Gillespie's China pony. Lindeman quickly secured a good position, and, riding well, beat the lot in the straight by several lengths amidst

great cheering. The victory for Australia was a highly popular one, especially amongst the British officers. The same evening the New South Wales officers at Chang Wang Palace dined with General Sir Norman Stewart and his staff. Sub-Lieutenant B. Black, located at the Llama Temple, has been appointed for the time being Police Commissioner in that district.

Sydney readers were thus assured that a certain 'ton' had returned to Peking now that things had settled down.

16

IN AID OF THE CIVIL POWER

Rape was not an offence, a pastime;
murder of the Chinese, an entertainment.

— Denis & Peggy Warner
'The Tide at Sunrise'

MUNICIPAL duties in Peking were not to everyone's liking, and the view was frequently expressed by the New South Wales contingent that they had not come all this way to be used as policemen and other non-military personnel.

One job that had to be undertaken was that of fire fighting. The chaos of the past months had quite destroyed what local rudimentary organisation there might have been and so, primarily for their protection against arson, the fire brigade was reconstituted. In the Tartar City area the brigade was run by Lieutenant Spain, assisted by Midshipman Walker. Their equipment was primitive and the water supply deficient, but they did the best they could. The main method of coping with a fire was to pull down adjoining buildings and it is creditable that there were no large fires in their area. In areas of the city which were under the control of the other Powers large conflagrations were commonplace events.

Police and municipal matters were in the hands of two petty officers, Blacker and Adams. One of their duties was to control gambling by the Chinese and frequent raids were made on gambling dens. Although a number of alleged criminals were captured, these raids seem to have had little effect.

Sanitation was another matter. Teams of coolies were employed to clean up the streets in the Australian-run areas and the result was a marked improvement, perhaps due to the fact that litterers faced 50 lashes when caught.

A gang, described as burglars and highway robbers, was caught by the Australians in early December, when some of the police force raided a house at 5.00 a.m. using ladders to scale a 12-foot high wall. Later, having been flogged at the orders of a Chinese court to induce their confessions, the gang were kept in the police station to await their execution.

The British (and Australian) method of execution was amended at about this time from firing squad to decapitation, in the belief that, according to Chinese lights, the former method was but a comparatively minor punishment. Perhaps so, but the effect on the recipient seems to have been similar.

But this arbitrary administration of justice occasionally misfired. In early December the headquarters of the New South Wales contingent at Chang-wang fu received orders to raid a large house in their area which belonged to a prominent Boxer. The furniture was to be taken to the British Legation, where it was badly needed. What was left was to be regarded as loot. No sooner said than done, and the equal distribution of the spoils occupied a couple of days. The loot, which included furs, silks and 'rare china' was auctioned amongst the officers and the proceeds — over $350 Mexican — was distributed to the men. As the payout concluded orders were received to return everything. They had raided the wrong house, and should have ransacked the one next door. The incident was not taken at all well by any of the participants.

A squad of the New South Wales police force with their mascot, Peking 1900. The ratings are armed with rifles and the two petty officers with revolvers.

As a diversion from these little embarrassments, the officers had recourse to the newly opened Peking International Club. The opening night, according to Wynne, 'was a swagger institution, and uniformed officers from all Allied forces filled the main hall from end to end. The liquor bill for the opening ceremony ran into £200, which is sufficient to indicate that 'the proceedings were marked by considerable enthusiasm'.

Social arrangements for the ratings fell somewhat short of those for the officers. There do not seem to have been any wet canteen arrange-

ments and as a consequence many resorted to local shanties and beer shops in search of a drink. Beer was difficult to obtain, and the main alternative was the raw Chinese spirit distilled from rice and called 'Samshu'. Literally, this is shao jiu, 'the wine that burns', from personal experience an apt name. Wynne informed his readers:

A gill can be bought from a Chinaman for about 5 cash, roughly ½d. It does not take many gills to make a man temporarily mad. Four or five of our men have experienced to their sorrow the effects of this vile stuff. Now

107

Lieutenant General Sir Alfred Gaselee calls on the headquarters of the New South Wales contingent at the Chang-wang Palace in 1901. Captain Gillespie sits next to him, with Commander Connor on his left.

the men are strictly forbidden to drink it under severe penalties and the Chinamen have also been warned not to sell or they will lose their licence and be flogged.

The feeling of isolation following the closing of the river supply route, due to ice, was dissipated somewhat by the opening at the beginning of December of the railway line between Peking and Tientsin. The service was slow and erratic and was, initially, in the hands of the Russians before being handed back to the British operators later in the month.

This development only improved communication between the two cities, as the Russian icebreakers at Taku had given up their task and had returned to Port Arthur leaving the port inaccessible until spring. The section of the line which ran from the mouth of the Pei Ho to the port of Shan-hai-kwan, which remained ice-free, was not yet open as the Russians were still

repairing it. The delay, though unavoidable due to the amount of damage the Chinese had done to the track and bridges, did negate the headlong dash to secure the Peitang forts in September.

Any thoughts that the situation was so peaceful that Messrs Yuill's sword would be only carried in future for the cutting of wedding cakes by its owner Bertie Black were dispelled by an expedition which took place not long before Christmas. Sub-Lieutenant Black, stationed at the Llama temple, heard from an informant that there was a cache of buried treasure in a town about twenty miles north of Peking. The amount of the treasure was estimated at 200 000 taels (£30 000) by Wallace and 'millions' by Wynne. Its existence was reported to Colonel Tulloch, who was not only the officer in command of the Baluchistan regiment but also the president of the prize fund.

The train service re-opened between Tientsin and Peking at the beginning of December 1900. The photograph shows three of the coaches near the newly opened terminus inside the main city wall. The old terminus outside the wall at Ma-chia-pu had been destroyed by the Boxers after the seige had started. As may be seen from the size of the coaches, the railway was a comparatively modest affair.

According to the informant the treasure was the property of 'a Boxer of the worst brand'. For a consideration he was willing to show where it was hidden.

The result was an expedition to secure the treasure. The party consisted of 25 men of the Baluchis, under the command of the Colonel, with Bertie Black invited to accompany the detachment presumably as a consequence of the information he had given. Their target was the 'prosperous, well-kept' village of Chang-hsin-chuang, and they set off, taking some carts into which to put the booty, through the Antingmen (gate) at the north-east corner of the city wall at daybreak.

They came under minor sniper fire as they left the city, but dispersed it with a volley and

by noon had reached their destination, where they started their mid-day meal before getting down to the business of digging. As they ate, their informant asked permission to go on to the next town, Kao-li-ying, because he had heard of a much bigger hoard of treasure there. Permission was granted and off he set.

Later that day they heard of his fate. He had been cut to pieces by irate Chinese who blamed him for the presence of the troops. Hearing of this, Tulloch set off with his men in the direction of Kao-li-ying the next morning and came under fire from the walls of the town as they approached. Fire was returned and the town entered, where the head man and a wealthy pawnbroker were told that because the troops were fired on the town would be razed

From left to right: Sub-Lieutenant Bertie Black, the proud owner of Messrs Yuill's sword; Lieutenant Hixson; Midshipman Bracegirdle and Asst Paymaster Wynne.

unless a fine of 35 000 taels (£5350) was paid. The force then departed, taking the two Chinese as hostages.

Reports were received that a mob of Boxers was gathering to attack them. Tulloch sent for reinforcements, who were soon on their way in the shape of 50 more Baluchis under a Lieutenant McPherson. A combined assault was made at 3.00 a.m. on the town and the supposed 'Boxers' routed, with an estimated 40 of their number being killed. The town was partially razed and a start had been made with a frantic search for the buried treasure when an order to return to Peking immediately came from a horrified General Gaselee. The party left so quickly that most of the ransom money had to be left behind.

The only reason for the episode was the search for loot. Present-day treasure-seekers may be discouraged by the fact that Peking International Airport covers most of the land under which the treasure was alleged to be buried.

The matter of looting has so far been raised mainly with treasure alleged to belong to Boxers. It is perhaps an appropriate stage to consider what may have been in the minds of some of the volunteers in Sydney, Melbourne and Adelaide, in particular those who had served on board a man-of-war on the China Station of the Royal Navy: plunder and its bed-mate, prize money. The Chinese military philosopher Sun-tze put the matter in a nutshell when he said: 'The soldiers must have their rewards so that they can see the advantage of defeating the enemy.'

By the end of 1900 the North China Plain in general, and the Taku—Tientsin—Peking—Pao-ting fu areas in particular, had been very thoroughly plundered by several expert teams. The Boxers had been on the rampage, and the Imperial Chinese Army had succeeded them in their depredations of town and country alike. The armed forces of the invaders had been narrowly preceded by the local citizens taking advantage of the breakdown of what little law and order had existed.

As Denis and Peggy Warner say in their book *The Tide at Sunrise:*

> . . . The allies made the most of it [Peking]. The Summer Palace, rebuilt after it had been sacked by the British and the French, was no exception. The Japanese went for the Treasury and seized three million taels of pure silver and the government silk and rice stores. The British treated it like an official auction sale . . . The Germans sacked the Imperial Observatory and shared the plunder with the French. For weeks the looting and destruction went on . . .

No wonder, then, that the Australian contingents' late arrival on the scene was a matter of regret in more ways than one. Not only had they missed the fighting with a chance of the attendant glory, but they had missed the best loot.

The usual explanation for the behaviour of the Allied forces is that it was all part of going to war: the Chinese were doing it, as were the armies of the other countries involved, so why shouldn't they. These activities led to a certain amount of pious editorialising. The *Sydney Morning Herald*, normally in the forefront of moral causes, for some reason had to resort on this occasion to borrowing an article from the *San Francisco Chronicle* to express its views second hand:

> The campaign to Peking has been a carnival of loot. Stores, temples, palaces, hovels have been stripped of their stocks and furnishings by the avenging allied armies, and there is not a soldier's haversack that is not weighted with Oriental treasure. Bayonets and butts of rifles have forced doors and windows, and walls have gone down before sledges and powder. There have been efforts to check this wild game of free looting, but in most instances they have been futile.

The *Chronicle* continued smugly:

> The Americans have been the most temperate of all, but General Chaffee [their commander] found it necessary to permit his men to forage and the American hand has gone nearly as far as any into the loot pile.

Perhaps considering the problems of transporting the object back to Australia — officers from the New South Wales contingent in the Forbidden City, Peking 1901.

The Allied commander-in-chief was less partisan. 'Every nationality,' said Count von Waldersee, 'accords the palm to some other in respect to the art of plundering, but it remains the fact that each and all of them went in hot and strong for loot.'

The only amendment that might be necessary to his views is that, in a particularly sordid aspect of a not very edifying military incident, the first prize for wanton pillage and destruction was unanimously awarded by the others to the Russian troops.

The few personal records that exist today are reticent on the subject of individual items brought back to Australia by the contingents as trophies or mementos of their time in China. One report which appeared in the now long-defunct *Town and Country Journal* of 1 December 1900 quotes one of the Victorian contingent as saying that the 'Australians will participate in the loot obtained at Tientsin, amongst which is 150 tons of silver', but that particular item seems to have been an early example of a furphy. Certainly there were sales of official loot, legally — if that is the correct word — obtained and disposed of, and Able Seaman Bertotto mentions two 'share-outs', one amounting to 3.25 Mexican dollars and the other, obtained during the expedition to Pao-ting fu, of a sum he omits to mention.

At the other end of the scale, both socially and in scope, according to a British officer, in October 'Lady MacDonald [the wife of the British Minister in Peking] was out with a small force left behind in Peking and devoted herself most earnestly to looting'.

In connection with the Kao-li-ying incident General Gaselee made his disapproval formal by later issuing orders to the British China Field Force that he would not approve the dispatch of expeditions unless they were provoked by some special act of hostility.

17

INTO 1901

By the beginning of December the contingent of Victorians in Tientsin, like their colleagues in Peking, had virtually ceased to exist as a formed military body and their strength as a fighting unit had also been dissipated by the demands of police work and other municipal chores. Added to these, as the weeks went by, were several other supplementary tasks and men were detailed to be train guards and ticket collectors now that the Tientsin/Taku section was in British hands.

Their battle effectiveness is of course open to debate as they had never fought an action. From the admittedly limited evidence available it is by no means clear whether they had had more than the most elementary field training since landing in China. For the remainder of their time in the country there was a succession of little jobs to be carried out, some of which were probably of a 'make work' nature.

Recreation facilities were almost nonexistent and the men had to make their own entertainment. Able Seaman Bertotto tells of an evening spent at the German military hospital, where he and two chums spent a very enjoyable time telling and hearing of experiences in different parts of the country, doubtless with suitable embellishments, and, after supper and grog, returned to quarters at midnight.

At an inspection in the middle of the month, the British General Lorne Campbell praised the contingent for their clean and comfortable quarters. The most obvious explanation for this high standard probably lies in the fact that the men were older and more settled. Many had been in the Royal Navy and had thus learned to look after themselves and some, having come from civilian occupations, probably contained in their numbers many tradesmen and family men to whom 'fixing up' came naturally.

The clearest indication that they were no longer regarded as a fighting force was the trans-

The Astor House Hotel, Tientsin. The building eventually extended beyond this 1984 photograph and became the Tientsin Hotel; at present undergoing an extensive and long-overdue renovation.

The New South Wales contingent parading one of their 12-pounders with ponies harnessed to the traces.

fer, on 26 December, of their 12-pounder guns to their counterparts in Peking. For some obscure military bureaucratic reason Christmas Day was spent getting them ready for dispatch by train under their guard.

The New Year was ushered in in Tientsin by yet another Review, this time of all British troops. It was held on New Year's Day, and was followed by an international concert, at which three military bands, French, American and Australian, performed. 'We had songs and music in ten languages, so we had a variety and kept going until midnight,' as Able Seaman Bertotto records. The officers fared somewhat better, with a dinner that evening hosted by the British general at the Astor House Hotel to celebrate the founding of the Commonwealth. Correspondent Wallace, who was at the dinner, preserved the menu shown in the right column.

The band played eight selections, including piccolo and clarinet solos, and two encores.

In Peking, as 1900 drew to a close most of the contingent's energies seem to have been directed towards matters equine: teams of mules for the 12-pounders had been trained, most of

Oxtail Soup

Fish, horseradish sauce

Chicken Patties

Saddle of Mutton
(French Beans, Green Peas, Potatoes)

Hare Callops, Mashed Chestnuts

Truffled Turkey, Salad, Stewed Fruit

Plum Pudding, Mince Pies

Welsh Rarebit

Fruit   Coffee

the officers and many of the men had mounts, and mounted patrols were quite frequent. The availability of ponies led, inevitably, to their being trained to pull the guns and limbers in place of sailor power.

Their first public appearance was at the fourth Peking Gymkhana, held at an impromptu track at the Temple of Heaven. Six of the ponies were entered, with their riders, in the gun mule race, but were beaten by a similar

The New South Wales contingent's artillery may have been getting ready for the international competition held in Peking in early 1901. Note the comparatively small size of the ponies.

team from the Bengal Lancers. The Australians' ace jockey, Sub-Lieutenant Lindeman, failed to maintain his earlier form and was beaten in the pony race by a Major Climo.

Professional honour was restored in an indirect way a few days later when the contingent took part in an artillery display competition. The exercise involved bringing down fire on a concentration of 'enemy' who then obligingly retreated. The artillery batteries then had to advance and open fire on the 'enemy's' new position. The other batteries participating were the 12th Battery Royal Field Artillery and the 5th American Field Battery.

The Australians did well in the shooting part of the competition but were not so impressive in the movement of their guns over the terrain, coming some way behind the R.F.A. Still, there was a bright side to this. As Wallace says: 'We were proud of our comrade's shooting, and we were proud, too, of the way in which the British battery covered the ground, perhaps partly because every animal in the gun teams was a "Waler".' The reference was to Australian horses which were regularly exported to India and other countries in Asia during the nine-

teenth and early part of the twentieth century. The majority of these came from New South Wales. They enjoyed a deserved reputation for reliability and staying power. Many were used in Hong Kong as race horses well into this century.

By this time the contingent seems to have collected, by some strange alchemy, a number of Indian camp followers. Language differences occurred. Wallace again.

... we get along somehow. 'Sahib', 'deeko', 'jerriwaller', are all we can make of the lengthy harangues to which the dusky Indians treat us occasionally, but if we don't understand them, we make sure they understand us. 'Get my horse saddled, Jones,' said an officer to his servant, and as he approached the stables a few minutes later he was astonished to hear the bluejacket yell. 'Hi! there! deeko, jerriwaller, Murrumbidgee, Cootamundra, Bondi, Alexandria; I can't speak your blankey lingo, but if you don't saddle this horse durned quick, I can break your dusky jaw, and I'll do it.' In less than no time the job was done, and Jones led the saddled steed into the courtyard still muttering highly-colored threats.

The New South Wales contingent had several Maxim machine guns in Peking. Here is a detachment setting off from barracks, observed by a number of Chinese civilians.

Christmas passed in Peking in much the same way as it did in Tientsin, with presumably much the same thoughts of home in Australia. The news which circulated a few days later was therefore of much interest to all. The contingents would be returning to Australia as soon as the winter broke and the port of Taku opened for shipping in the new year. This was normally some time in March, so there were only another ten or so weeks to go.

The obligatory New Year's Day parade had, in 1901, an additional significance for the British Empire. Apart from being the anniversary of the proclamation of Queen Victoria as Empress of India in 1877 and thus of significance to the Indians, this year there was also the celebration of the federation of the Australian states into the Commonwealth.

In Peking, fully 2000 British (including Australian) troops took part and the New South Wales contingent, mustering two companies, headed the infantry brigade. Lieutenant Lofts' marines formed the guard of honour of the national flag. Lieutenant-General Sir A. Gaselee cabled congratulations to the new country from Peking, noting that Australia 'has so

opportunely assisted here with a valuable contingent'.

The officers of the contingent had a busy social day, being entertained to lunch at the International Club by the Commander-in-Chief and dinner by the commander of the 1st Brigade, of which they were part. Wynne reports the proceedings as 'being of a most enthusiastic and patriotic character throughout'. No record exists of the activities of the sailors of the contingents in either Peking or Tientsin on Federation Day, 1901.

General Gaselee either had a change of heart or a bout of influenza affected his judgement, because of few days later he authorised a second expedition to the 'notorious Boxer centre of Kao-li-ying'.

The second force sent out, this time with the task of recovering the ransom money abandoned earlier (some £5250), was again under Tulloch's command, but was somewhat larger than the first detachment. It consisted of 100 Japanese, about 350 Baluchis and Sikhs and 26 men of the New South Wales contingent under Lieutenant Staunton Spain.

The force's orders were to collect the fine. If

they were unsuccessful, they were to destroy the town. No mention was made of any search for the mythical buried treasure whose presence had prompted the first expedition. The town was reached on the second day of heavy marching through the snow. Not surprisingly, the place was almost deserted, most of the inhabitants having disappeared, together with any hope of recovering the fine.

The troops were billeted in some deserted houses overnight, and the next morning it was decided to destroy the large Buddhist temple in the town. The reasons for doing this were, according to Wallace:

> ... it had been the headquarters for the Boxer movement in the district and contained several torture chambers or 'hells'. The walls of these chambers were covered with large scrolls depicting, after the manner of Chinese art, the gruesome and horrible tortures which there is every reason to believe were carried out in the place quite recently. The large idols were smashed to pieces, the worshipping paraphernalia scattered to the winds, and then the adjacent buildings were pulled down and others blown up with gunpowder to prevent the whole town catching fire. During this operation a Sikh had his leg broken. Several charges of gun-cotton were drilled into the temple, the more inflammable parts soaked with kerosene — a large supply having been discovered in the town — and then the troops were ordered out of danger. One by one the charges were exploded, the temple was soon in ruins, and its entire destruction completed when the woodwork caught fire.

There was a scheme to blow up the main gate of the town and the charges had already been laid when a German force of about 300 hove into view, bound on some other punitive errand. As they wanted to use the town for a while the task of destroying the gate was left to them. Honour having been satisfied (according to the rules of engagement prevailing in North China in 1901), the British force returned across the snow to their barracks in Peking. Wynne, with a final word:

> The good behaviour of the bluejackets throughout was complimentarily commented on by Lieutenant-Colonel Tulloch when reporting what the expedition had done ... they make home seem fairer than it did when an honest fight with a worthy foe was promised. We now know that there's no work here for men, and we are counting the days that separate us from Australia.

18

RUNNING DOWN

THE 1901 version of R & R for the Victorian contingent started in the new year. Able Seaman Bertotto and a group were on a trip to Peking which started on 22 January when they took the train to the capital, being quartered at the New South Wales contingent's headquarters at Chang-wang fu. They were, Connor sourly notes in his diary, having seen either them or another group, 'a rough lot'.

Their first day of sightseeing included the Temple of a Thousand Years outside the Tartar City in the morning and the Summer Palace in the afternoon, travelling in panchaus, native carts with wooden wheels and no springs. At the Summer Palace they visited the marble barge and most of the 'state' rooms: '... the furniture being a sight not to be forgotten, all splendid carvings in marble, bronze and wood ... I managed to get away with a carved panel which I took off a sideboard.' They returned to barracks for the night.

Next day they set off early in the morning, first visiting the Great Llama Temple, to see: '... instruments of torture, a great many of which had been used quite recently, as blood and hair of some unlucky beings still adhered to them.' Bertotto 'borrowed' a silver bronze bell six inches long and five inches diameter at the mouth.

The next port of call was the British Legation, where '... it seemed as if the whole fire of the besiegers had been poured into this place as there was not a brick or a stone that was not marked with a shot ...' On next to the For-

bidden City, where Bertotto commented on the quality of the carving and size of the marble pieces, in particular: '... two large marble columns about 40 feet high and about 8 feet diameter at the base and had a dragon carved spirally on them and on the top was a peacock. The most striking features of these columns were that each one was only one piece of marble.' On return to barracks they were informed of the death of Queen Victoria; the news had taken two days to reach Peking from London. Able Seaman Bertotto seems to have remained unaffected.

The following day they set off bright and early to visit the Temple of Heaven, followed by the Peking Observatory, where '... there were a great many instruments, some very queer looking ones, all made of bronze'. They met a party of Japanese and together climbed Coal Hill, a vantage point with a very good view of the city '... which looked very pretty in the sunlight, all the roofs of the buildings being of tiles of the Imperial colour: yellow'. (As they are still.) The day ended with a visit to the Roman Catholic cathedral, which had also been besieged in a less publicised but possibly more gallant and energetic episode at the same time as the Legations. The five days' sightseeing itinerary does not differ markedly from that of the modern tourist.

Back to Tientsin for the group, and preparation for the next ceremonial, which was to be the memorial service for the late Queen, held on Saturday 2 February.

The Memorial parade marking the death of Queen Victoria, Peking 1901. Units of the British Field Force, China, are paraded in front of the Wu Men — the Meridian Gate — of the Forbidden City.

The service was held in the open, with about two feet of snow on the ground, and the thermometer 3 degrees below zero [Fahrenheit, one assumes]. We were obliged to stand with 'arms reversed' for an hour and three quarters, so we felt the cold keenly, and were not sorry when it was finished.

By now it was mainly a matter of hanging on for the weeks that remained before the river would be navigable and they could get away. For one of the New South Wales contingent though this was too long. Able Seaman Eli Rose, from Newcastle, died of pleurisy in the middle of January and was buried in the British cemetery alongside Staff-Surgeon Steel.

February slipped by slowly for the two contingents, uninterrupted by any real excitements. The Chinese, now that the Allies were apparently more intent on peace negotiations than revenge, were becoming increasingly bold in their attitude to the temporary occupiers.

As the Allied troops approached the eastern walls of Peking the previous August the Empress Dowager had escaped to the west, together with the Emperor Kuang-hsu and a few attendants. Their flight ended all semblance of government in China, and it was eventually left to the elder Chinese statesman of the nineteenth century, Li Hung-chang, to make his way to the capital from Canton, in the far south of the country, to start peace negotiations.

Li arrived in Tientsin in September, but the talks to establish peace were very slow in starting and, when they did, dragged on for month after month. The main provisions concerned the punishment of the high officials involved in the uprising and the size of the indemnity. By the middle of February it was clear that there was to be no more large scale fighting in northern China and the foreign troops could be safely withdrawn.

The last few weeks of the Australian contingents' stay in China were not very edifying.

The Chinese elder statesman of the nineteenth century, Li Hung-chang, who was responsible for the Chinese side in the peace negotiations.

Lieutenant Lindeman carried out a mounted patrol in the middle of February 1901. His 'Ocean Dragoons' went after bandits, but all they found was a Chinese funeral. Lieutenant Spain may have captured them setting out on this patrol in this photograph and the photograph below.

The China Steam Navigation Company's SS Chingtu, which became Transport 106 *for the voyage carrying the contingents back to Australia in 1901.*

This was the result of a long winter, boredom and inactivity, coupled with 'going-home fever.' However, as far as can be ascertained from the accounts which still exist, their conduct was much better than that of the other troops.

In his book *The World's Navies in the Boxer Rebellion* (*China 1900*), written in 1905, Lieutenant C.C. Dix, Royal Navy, refers to 'the efficient police work carried out by the Australian sailors'.

Writing in mid-February for his contemporary *Herald* readers, John Wallace asserts that the health of the contingents was excellent with no one in hospital following the discharge of Able Seaman Walsh, who had recovered from an attack of smallpox '... although his face shows the ravages of the disease'. The Germans were particularly badly off as far as sickness was concerned, with over 200 in hospital in Tientsin.

Bickering and fighting amongst the different nationalities started to occur, although not apparently directly involving the Australians. Small scandals were reported, the following account doubtless edited for the sensitive *Herald* readers.

A terrible tragedy was enacted last week in the only hotel in Peking, when a young Danish officer, Captain Linberg, formerly employed as military instructor to the Chinese troops at Tientsin, shot his wife dead with his revolver.

He then wounded Lieutenant Denning, of the 3rd Bombay Cavalry, over the left hip, and finally committed suicide by shooting himself through the right temple. The murdered lady was a Dane, of attractive appearance, about 28 years of age, and she had journeyed to Peking with Lieutenant Denning. Jealousy is said to be the only cause assigned for the terrible tragedy. Lieutenant Denning lies in a critical condition, and is being nursed by one of our contingent.

One sweep was undertaken into the British area south of Peking in the middle of February by ten of the New South Wales contingent under the command of that noted horseman Lieutenant Lindeman. As might have been expected the patrol, which was part of a larger force, was a mounted one, and Lieutenant Spain may have recorded their muster and departure in the photographs shown on page 121.

The task of the patrol was a consequence of Chinese villagers' requests for protection from 'banditti' and a handful of Chinese Christian converts who were said to be terrorising the countryside. The 'Ocean Dragoons', as they were styled, rode Chinese ponies. They only had one chance to demonstrate their horsemanship. 'Away on the skyline a large body of Chinese was observed moving along. "The banditti," exclaimed an officer, (presumably Lindeman) and the next minute the sailors were helter skelter across the country in hot pursuit' . . . of what turned out to be a Chinese funeral.

The Emperor of Japan's birthday on 11 February was the occasion for the Japanese contingent in Tientsin to hold what Able Seaman Bertotto calls a 'banyan'. This is a term still current in the Royal Australian Navy, now used to describe a party when sailors from a ship anchored offshore go ashore to cook a meal and drink beer on a deserted tropical beach.

> We were treated to the best of everything, the whole of the Japanese quarter of the town was illuminated with Japanese lanterns of all possible colours. Music by all nationalities, abundance of food of all kinds, sweets, saki and dancing and a gordgeos display of fireworks. We enjoyed ourselves immensely until the small hours of the morning, then we returned to our respective quarters, well satisfied.

A few days later he was detailed to join a team to patrol the river banks and was in a good position to report, towards the end of February, that the ice was starting to break up. This was the news they had all been waiting for: it indicated that they would soon be on their way back to Australia.

First, though, there was the matter of their replacement. Originally they were meant to be replaced by a battalion of the Devons, who were making their way to China from the United Kingdom. As their troopship passed the Cape, an upturn in the fighting there had caused them to be landed in South Africa instead, delaying their arrival in China. Four companies of the Royal Welsh Fusiliers were dispatched to northern China from Hong Kong, which cannot have pleased them greatly, as they had only had a few months in the colony since their time in the north the previous year.

That, however, was not the Australians' problem; their departure had been set for the end of March in the China Navigation Company's SS *Chingtu*, a steamer of 2300 tons.

19

SECURE

MEANWHILE, there were still alarms and excursions ·to be dealt with by the Victorians in Tientsin. The first was the Affair of Kinder's Siding, on the east bank of the river at Tientsin.

The incident was an armed confrontation between the British and Russians from 14 March, over a strip of land on which Mr Kinder, a British engineer, was building a siding to the Peking–Tientsin–Taku railway. The Russians maintained that the land was part of a new concession granted to them and the British disagreed. The Victorians were placed in readiness to back up the Sikh and Hong Kong Regiments. Sixty men of the New South Wales contingent, with Connor at their head, were also rushed down from Peking to act as reinforcements. According to Able Seaman Bertotto, who was involved, the British could only muster 1900 men in the fighting line while the Russian force was over 6000. Diplomatic efforts averted an outbreak of hostilities between the Allied troops and the Russians backed down.

While the Victorians were across the Pei Ho backing up the Sikhs, a mutiny broke out among the French troops in Tientsin. Things got so bad during the day that General Campbell called out the Bombay Lancers and Bengal Cavalry to clear the streets. No one was killed but several were wounded.

This was the most serious incident in what was fast becoming a general breakdown in discipline among the foreign troops in Tientsin and, to a lesser extent, in Peking. In Tientsin the Victorian sailor-police had many scrapes with foreign troops, particularly with the French, who drew their bayonets and attacked at the slightest provocation. Several of the contingent were wounded, though none seriously.

On 23 March, Able Seaman Bertotto records in his diary the arrival in Tientsin of Lighter No. 8, under the tow of the tug *Hai-hu*, carrying 420 men of the 2nd Battalion Royal Welsh Fusiliers, from Hong Kong via Shanghai.

All was now ready for their departure. The farewell parades had taken place, the speeches were all over. The Australians' thoughts were now all directed on their return. For the majority it was a pleasant prospect; for some it was one that was to be deferred for a while. The railway company had asked for volunteers from both contingents to remain behind for several months to assist in the running of the line. The terms offered were 10s per day, clothing, food and accommodation provided and a free passage back to Australia on completion of their contract. Seventeen New South Wales men volunteered. The Taku Tug and Lighterage Company offered similar contracts, with acceptances from two Victorians.

The prospect of return proved too much altogether for one man. In Peking, Able Seaman Bennett was discovered one evening 'lying quite dead on the floor of his quarters face downward in a pool of blood'. The deceased's rifle was lying on the floor 2 feet away, the muzzle pointing towards him, and there was an empty cartridge case in the chamber. A Court of Inquiry

The Kinder's siding affair, Tientsin 1901. Russian and British (Indian Army) troops have an eyeball-to-eyeball confrontation over a strip of disputed land on which a Mr Kinder wanted to build a railway siding.

Another view of the Kinder's siding affair from the Russian side. The Victorian contingent had to stop their packing to go back to Australia and stand by in case hostilities broke out between Britain and Russia. 60 men of the New South Wales contingent were also sent down from Peking to act as reinforcements. The whole affair eventually blew over.

This photograph possibly shows the New South Wales contingent loading a train in Peking with their baggage ready to be sent to Taku and then to be stowed on board the Chingtu.

consisting of two Indian Army officers and Sub-Lieutenant Black heard evidence that Bennett had '. . . been ailing for some time. He had complained of pains in the head, and could not sleep.' The Court found that he died from a wound self-inflicted whilst in an unsound state of mind. He left a widow and several children. Connor gives us a little more detail. Three weeks earlier he had disrated Bennett from petty officer 2nd class to able seaman for being drunk on duty and assault on a chief petty officer. 'I fancy his disrating had unhinged his brain — anyhow it's all very sad.'

The Victorians handed over to the Royal Welsh Fusiliers and stowed all their gear aboard Lighter No. 8 on the morning of 25 March.

Their departure was delayed by another parade and inspection by their general, who complimented them on their work and behaviour while under his command. They gave three cheers all round, passed the towline to the tug *Heron* which had towed them up the river seven months previously, then set off down towards the open sea. They spent the night at the British base at Hsin-ho and boarded the *Chingtu*, *Transport 106*, at 9.00 the next morning. Rough weather at the bar delayed the arrival and embarkation of the New South Wales contingent until 29 March. As Able Seaman Bertotto says in the final, laconic, entry in his diary: 'We could now look to the West and to the land in the distance and say "Good Bye" North China.'

126

20

PIPE DOWN

THE thoughts of all onboard the *Chingtu*, as the ship made her way down the China coast, must have been turning to their reception back in Sydney and Melbourne, not only from the civic authorities but also from their wives and families. All had personal souvenirs of differing value in their baggage; in addition the contingent had two official trophies to be presented to the government. One was a bronze cannon, 10 feet long and weighing two tons, carrying a date of 1595 and an inscription showing it to be a present from Phillip II of Spain to the Chinese. It is now at the main gate of Garden Island Dockyard in Sydney. The other was a large bronze bell, beautifully engraved and said to be well over 300 years old.

The whereabouts of this bell — or gong — remains a mystery. Certainly the one hanging outside the Wardroom at HMAS *Penguin* (a) has a good claim; however it seems to be of a different size and pattern to the one being rolled along by a team of coolies (b) in China before the voyage to Australia. The Australian War Memorial lays claim to a third gong (c).

The contingent did not carry back the 12-pounder quick-firing guns exchanged in Hong Kong for the obsolete artillery brought with them from Australia the previous year. When the *Chingtu* stopped in Hong Kong, the Australians were reminded by the Royal Navy there that the guns had only been on loan and that theirs were ready to be collected from the armament depot.

One man was also left behind, Signalman Walsh, who, perhaps through being drunk, missed the ship and returned to Australia later. Two men, both sick, had been left in China — Able Seaman Tom Arnsby, recovering in

The bronze cannon presented to the Australian government as an official trophy of the contingents' activities in China. It is at the Main Gate of the Royal Australian Navy's Garden Island Dockyard, Sydney.

(a) *A bronze bell, a trophy of the contingent's activities in China 1900–1901. It may not be the official trophy presented to the Australian government in recognition of the contingents' activities.*

(c) *Another claimant to the description of the bronze bell brought back from China by the contingents. This one is in the Australian War Memorial in Canberra.*

(b) *A gang of coolies with the Chinese bell or gong presented to the Australian government to commemorate the activities of the naval contingents in China 1900–1901.*

The United States Navy's battleship USS Oregon, in Hong Kong, April 1901.

A parade on board the Chingtu *returning from China in 1901 with the Australian contingents on board. Note the birds in the cages.*

hospital in Peking from enteric and brain fever, and the pier-head jumper Private Ferns in Tientsin suffering from German measles. Both returned to Australia later.

While in Hong Kong Midshipman Murnin noted the United States Navy's battleship USS *Oregon* in harbour and Lieutenant Spain took a photograph of the ship.

The *Chingtu* sailed from Hong Kong on 5 April 1901, setting course for Thursday Island, to embark fresh meat and water. Connor noted in his diary, 'Something is wrong with the speed of the *Chingtu*. The engineers opine that there is something wrong with the propeller, perhaps a blade gone.' Five days out from Hong Kong he notes 'The men apparently want to make themselves felt — making an awful row and quite out of hand for about ½ hour till the Captain straightened them up a bit. The Petty

Officers are afraid of doing their work.'

Their planned arrival in Sydney was reported by a telegram from Thursday Island on 18 April. It did not appear to create much in the way of an increased beat to the civic heart, although in an announcement the New South Wales Premier, Sir William Lyne, said it had been decided to give the members of the contingent a hearty welcome home. This was to amount to a march through the streets to the Drill Hall, and before their disbanding he would make a short address.

The effect of this munificent municipal welcome was not immediately tested. The Public Health authorities were informed three days before the ship's planned arrival in Port Jackson that she had sailed from Thursday Island under quarantine. An exchange of messages between the ship and the signal station

The officers of the Victorian contingent on board the Chingtu on their way back to Australia, 1901. Commander Tickell has his summer uniform buttoned up the correct way on this occasion. The Captain and First Officer of the Chingtu are also included in the photograph.

A group of the first and second-class petty officers of the New South Wales contingent on board Chingtu April 1901.

Transport 106, *SS Chingtu, in the quarantine anchorage, North Head, Sydney, 1901. The ship had returned from China with a case of smallpox on board.*

on South Solitary Island confirmed that the *Chingtu* did not have a clean bill of health and would be entering Sydney with the quarantine flag flying. Corporal Symonds of the marine detachment was ill. As a result neither crew nor passengers would be permitted to land. There were no further details available in Sydney until the evening of 25 April, when at last the ship steamed through the Heads in the dark to the quarantine anchorage in the lee of North Head.

The naval brigade and band had been waiting at Circular Quay since early in the afternoon to welcome their comrades home, and friends and relatives of members of the contingent had gathered for the same purpose. They were all to be disappointed.

The next few days were ones of confusion. The ship remained anchored off the Quarantine Station at Sydney's North Head while the health authorities, having concluded that the sick man had in fact been suffering from a case of smallpox, from which he was now recovering, tried to check each member of the contingent to see if the vaccinations given them the

previous August were still effective. By stretching a point, for smallpox injections were meant to have a life of only six months in those days, it was possible for 146 of the New South Wales contingent and about 170 of the Victorians to be declared fit to land on Friday 3 May.

The decision was doubly gratifying to the Victorians who feared that, under the differing States' health rules, had they sailed to Melbourne in the *Chingtu* as originally planned they would have had to start their quarantine period all over again. The balance of the contingent, about 40 from New South Wales and twenty from Victoria, were re-vaccinated and landed at the Quarantine Station. This enabled the ship to take on a supply of coal and resume her normal cargo service, as she had been fumigated and declared free from disease. The unfortunates were forced to undergo a statutory period of fourteen days until they were cleared to enter Australia proper.

While they had been incarcerated on board the *Chingtu* waiting for permission to land, they had all been offered accommodation in the weatherboard quarters — which still stand —

This plaque was presented by the New South Wales contingent to the city of Sydney to commemorate the men who lost their lives on active service in China 1900–1901. The plaque is being presented here to the Flag Officer, East Australia Area, Vice Admiral Davidson, by the then Lord Mayor of Sydney Alderman Leo Port, for the Royal Australian Navy's safe keeping. The plaque is at present in the Dockyard Chapel, Garden Island Dockyard, Sydney.

The headstone to the grave in the cemetery at North Head, Sydney, of Private Smart of the New South Wales Marine Light Infantry, who died there of smallpox in 1901.

ashore at the Quarantine Station, but both the Victorians and the New South Wales men refused on discovering they would be separated from their baggage. This caused some perplexity among the civilians, but can be explained simply by considering the possible value of the contents of some of the kitbags. No prudent sailor was going to abandon his 'rabbits', as sailors call presents brought back from overseas, if at all possible.

At the last minute there was another case of sickness. Private C.W. Smart of the New South Wales Marine Light Infantry came down with what was soon diagnosed as a case of smallpox. He was removed to the hospital at North Head, where he subsequently died. Smart's name is recorded on a commemorative plaque given to Sydney by the members of the contingent. This plaque is now in the Garden Island Dockyard Chapel.

The more fortunate men were finally brought from the quarantine anchorage by lighter, together with their precious baggage, early in the morning of Friday 3 May and landed at Circular Quay at 10.15. They were met by the police band, many of their friends and relatives and a few of the naval brigade who had not gone to China. Forming up, they set off on a short march round the lower part of the city before doubling back to the Drill Hall at Fort Macquarie.

As far as can be ascertained from the newspaper accounts, the Victorians were left to their own devices. The next that is known of their movements is that they all caught the train that evening at Redfern station. They might not have minded being officially ignored by the politicians of New South Wales, as they were spared Sir William Lyne's harangue which was fulsome in the extreme. Eventually it was all over and the men were released after giving three cheers for the King, the Premier, Captain Gillespie and Commander Connor.

The Victorians returned to Melbourne on the evening of Saturday 4 April. The train fares from Albury amounted to £47 15s, being 190 ½ miles at 5d per man per mile. A final confusion arose when the train discharged its passengers at the Preston Dock platform; the crowds of welcomers were waiting at the main arrival platform at Spencer Street station. Due to the lateness of the hour there was no official reception and the men were re-united with their families without more ado.

The reservists from both brigades were soon discharged from service, receiving two months pay as a gratuity. But not before the Victorians had undergone a final parade, this time to be inspected by the Duke of York, who was making the first post-Federation Royal visit to Australia.

And so the episode ended, and the bluejackets all dispersed. The final words are best left to Bertotto, who was, after all, there at the time.

Nobody knows what happened to us, nobody knows or cares
Only those who fought old Kruger are allowed to put on airs
We had no crowd to see us off, no Mansion House invite
The bugle our only warning in the dead of a sultry night
Nobody cared when we landed, only those we came to save
But those we left behind us will ne'er have a stone to their graves
We were our own stretcher bearers, our own commisiriat too
And we didn't fight in a karki rig but in our own serge suits of blue
Our baggage followed close behind us, we had it on our backs
Our base of supply was never far off, it was in our haversacks
Donkeys and horses were mounts to us, or a mule of an unknown age
The rear rank found the bill-of-fare while the front rank found the range
Our grub was worse than Baden-Powell's even he served out a trifle more
But men who are used to starve at sea won't growl at the same ashore
We got no Tam-o'-Shanter caps, no chocolate in a box
No knitted stockings came our way, but we gave the 'Boxers' sox
Our guns went out at the gun-crews heels, and not in a railway train
But some of the crews are still alive and fit for the same again
We are back on board our ships again, back from the jaws of H — l
And the soldiers can finish the racket, We have cleared the road so well.

APPENDIX I

HMCS *Protector* Nominal Crew List

Most of the crew of HMCS Protector *photographed on board the cruiser before the ship sailed for China in 1900. Unfortunately there is no key to the group.*

SOUTH AUSTRALIA.

OFFICERS AND CREW OF "PROTECTOR" SENT TO CHINA.

Ordered by the House of Assembly to be printed, September 26th, 1900.

[Estimated cost of printing (650), £1 1s. 1d.]

NOMINAL LIST of OFFICERS and CREW of H.M.C.S. *PROTECTOR* DISPATCHED for SERVICE in CHINA.

NOMINAL LIST OF OFFICERS AND CREW OF H.M.C.S. *PROTECTOR* DISPATCHED FROM SOUTH AUSTRALIA ON AUGUST 6TH, 1900, FOR SERVICE IN CHINA.

Captain	William Rooke Creswell, R.N.
Senior Lieutenant	Captain Chapman James Clare
Lieutenant	Patrick Weir
Staff Engineer	William Clarkson
Chief Gunner	Edwin Argent
Gunner	John Denzil Turner
Boatswain	George Joss
Artificer Engineer	Robert Charles Duncan
Staff Surgeon	Bedlington Howell Morris
Paymaster	John Norton
succeeded by	
Assistant Paymaster	Ernest Claude Norton
(appointed August 14th, 1900)	
Interpreter	William H. Blake

1.	Petty Officer	John Winchester
2.	"	Rudolph Lucas
3.	"	Thomas Malloney
4.	Chief Armorer	Robert Sutherland
5.	Chief Stoker	Samuel Allen
6.	Leading Stoker	George Stuart
7.	Petty Officer	William Wood
8.	Engineer Artificer	George Deane
9.	A.B., First Class	George Luckett
10.	Steward	Charles E. Smith
11.	Cook's Mate	Jacob J. Davis
12.	Engineer Artificer	James Murison
13.	A.B., First Class	Alfred Mackay
14.	"	John Patterson Morrison
15.	"	William Thomas Edwards
16.	"	Bismark Johnson
17.	A.B., Second Class	John Gillis
18.	"	Robert Baker
19.	"	Joseph Silver
20.	"	John Carigliano
21.	"	John Norman
22.	Signalman	Arthur James Wooley
23.	Signal Petty Officer	Frank Vernon Woodman
24.	A.B., Second Class	George Frederick Jeffery
25.	A.B., First Class	John Henry Gill
26.	"	Alexander Scott Cameron
28.	"	Thomas Owen
29.	"	William Henry Brown
30.	"	Richard Beck
31.	"	William John Brown
32.	"	Richard Murch
33.	Petty Officer	James Gillespie
34.		
35.	A.B., First Class	Herbert Thomas Hill

36.	"	Herbert Henry Knowles
37.	"	John Healy
38.	"	James Halton
39.	Cook	Percival Turner
40.	A.B., First Class	Charles Thomas Carr
41.	"	John Clark Lamb
42.	A.B., First Class	Felix Charles Percival Carter
43.	A.B., Second Class	Frank Darmody
44.	Ordinary	Albert Stevens
45.	"	Edward O'Grady
47.	Petty Officer	James Barr
48.	A.B., First Class	Charles Ellis
50.	A.B., Second Class	James Ticklie
51.	"	William Henry Ticklie
52.	"	George Thornton
53.	"	Horace Lacerda
54.		
55.	Ordinary	Henry Thompson
56.	Boy, First Class	Harold Egbert Beare
57.	Petty Officer	John McEachern
58.	"	George Johnson
59.	A.B., Second Class	Arthur Joseph Onley
60.	Leading Stoker	Peter Robins
61.	Stoker	William Harris Austin
62.		
63.	Stoker	Samuel George Horricks
64.	"	Joseph Edward White
65.	"	Louis Johnson
66.	"	John Rogers
67.	"	William Hibbs
68.	"	Henry Lewis
69.	Leading Stoker	William Willis
70.	Petty Officer	Robert Smith
71.	"	Henry Perry
72.	Servant	Robert Duncan
73.	Leading Stoker	Henry McLean
74.	"	Robert Lloyd
75.	Stoker	George Shaw
76.	"	James John Hayter
77.	"	Robert Butler
78.	"	William Carr
79.	A.B., Second Class	John Burch
80.	Chief Petty Officer	Robert Fulton
81.	A.B., First Class	Louis Deers
82.	A.B., Second Class	David Alexander Ewen
83.	Servant	Robert Wylie
84.	A.B., First Class	Adam Smith Cameron
85.	Chief Carpenter's Mate ...	Samuel Jeanes
86.	A.B., First Class	Daniel Murphy

87. Petty Officer	George Garrison	
88. A.B., Second Class	Russel Grant	
89. Servant	Charles Smith	
90.		
91. A.B., First Class	George Perryman	
92. Ordinary	Andrew Neilson	
93. "	A. Moon	
94. Stoker	R. C. Aitkin	
95. Boy, First Class	R. W. Fenwick	
96. A.B., First Class	William Nicholls Batson	
97. "	Charles de Longville	
— Servant	F. Point	

The nominal list of the officers and men of the South Australian Navy's flagship HMCS *Protector* as published by the South Australian government. Chief Gunner Black is listed as an interpreter, which must have made him even more unhappy.

APPENDIX II

New South Wales Contingent

THE New South Wales contingent posed for their photographs after they had been enrolled in Sydney. These photographs are reproduced in the following pages.

An indication of the haste with which the contingent was raised is that a number of the men were not wearing uniform when their photographs were taken. Additionally, those who are wearing uniform are all dressed as able seamen. They were all initially enrolled as ABs and had the ratings they would hold in the contingent awarded later.

These 'beginning of term' photographs of the New South Wales contingent in 1900 have been taken from an illustrated weekly magazine of the time, the *Australian Town and Country Journal*.

"A" COMPANY.

Top row (reading from left to right): 1, W. Leslie (A.B.); 2, T. Conwell (A.B.); 3, G. W. Burgess (A.B.); 4, C. Boutell (A.B.); 5, J. C. Lindsell (A.B.); 6, A. Price (A.B.); 7, W. Laycock (A.B.); 8, J. H. Wills (A.B.); 9, ——; 10, A. Mackenzie (A.B.). Second row: 11, A. G. Shepherd (A.B.); 12, R. Young (A.B.); 13, G. L. Jones (A.B.); 14, G. Sharman (A.B.); 15, J. Wiggins (A.B.); 16, C. J. Larsen (A.B.); 17, F. Holloway (A.B.); 18, W. J. Lee (A.B.). Third row: 19, L. Bracegirdle (midshipman); 20, R. Cale (A.B.); 21, W. R. Parker (leading seaman); 22, P. W. Upton (A.B.); 23, F. W. Naylor (A.B.); 24, W. E. Woodcock (A.B.); 25, J. R. M'Farlane (A.B.); 26, J. M. Clinton (A.B.); 27, A. H. Sapsted (A.B.); 28, A. Geddes (A.B.); 29, A. E. Stone (A.B.); 30, ——; 31, J. Blacker (2nd P.O.); 32, C. Murnin (midshipman). Fourth row: 33, A. W. Ingram (A.B.); 34, E. Rose (A.B.); 35, A. T. Allen (A.B.); 36, J. Hood (A.B.); 37, J. Chester (A.B.); 38, D. W. Albone (A.B.); 39, F. D. Cryter (A.B.); 40, C. E. Whitley (A.B.); 41, T. F. Walker (A.B.). Bottom row: 42, T. Cahill (A.B.); 43, H. Payne (A.B.); 44, J. Pickering (A.B.); 45, G. J. Clarke (1st P.O.); 46, J. Walsh (signalman); 47, J. G. Sparkes (C.P.O.); 48, E. Madden (A.B.); 49, F. Whitwell (A.B.); 50, H. Arthur (leading seaman); 51, J. A. Nicholl (A.B.).

"B" COMPANY.

Top row (reading from left to right): 1 J. R. Bair (A.B.); 2 G. E. H. Dennis (A.B.); 3 H. M'Menemy (A.B.); 4 J. Reynolds (A.B.); 5 S. A. Kennedy (A.B.); 6 W. Smith (A.B.); 7 H. Jones (A.B.); 8 J. Ross (A.B.). Second row: 9 W. Surrenne (A.B.); 10 F. Buckley (A.B.); 11 W. E. Gould (A.B.); 12 A. H. Poole (A.B.); 13 V. Maloney (A.B.); 14 R. Thompson (A.B.); 15 W. Archibald (A.B.); 16 H. Coates (A.B.). Third row: 17 R. Dezochie (A.B.); 18 J. Pollard (A.B.); 19 A. Oliver (A.B.); 20 (Absent); 21 R. A. Buhl (A.B.); 22 W. Thomas (A.B.); 23 Warrant-Officer J. Rolfe; 24 Bugler F. Ballerein. Fourth row: J. Noble (A.B.); 26 S. A. Hearne (A.B.); 27 H. J. Hilliard (A.B.); 28 J. Good (A.B.); 29 C. Gray (A.B.); 30 H. Hilliard (A.B.); 31 R. M'Govern (A.B.); 32 J. Protheroe (A.B.); 33 D. Daggar (A.B.). Bottom row: 24 J. Hamilton (A.B.); 35 D. Farley (A.B.); 36 Treli (1); 37 Kingsford (1); 38 A. R. Reed (Leading Seaman); 39 G. Watson (A.B.); 40 M. Martell (A.B.); 41 J. Allen (C.P.O.); 42 J. Boddall (Signalman); 43 E. T. G. Puddephatt (1st P.O.); 44 J. Barnett (Leading Seaman); 45 A. J. Bennett (2nd P.O.); 46 J. Beynon (A.B.).

"C" COMPANY.

Top row (reading from left to right): 1, C. Hart (A.B.); 2, W. Giblin (A.B.); 3, C. Groves (A.B.); 4, H. Petts (A.B.); 5, H. J. May (A.B.); 6, J. Simpson (A.B.); 7, E. A. Chambers (A.B.); 8, R. H. Wright (signalman). Second row: 9 W. J. Elder (A.B.); 10, W. Watts (A.B.); 11, J. H. Jackson (A.B.); 12, F. Golden (A.B.); 13, W. Graham (A.B.); 14, H. J. Aird (A.B.); 15, W. C. Milton (A.B.). Third row: 16, R. S. Malone (C.P.O.); 17, W. J. Carr (A.B.); 18, J. Davis (A.B.); 19, J. Strugnell (A.B.); 20, J. H. Hughes (A.B.); 21, S. G. Troke (A.B.); 22, R. Flagman (A.B.); 23, M. A. Lodge (A.B.); 24, W. Hinnem (second-class P.O.); 25, H. Corben (L.S.); 26, H. Cooper (A.B.); 27, R. Garwood (A.B.); 28, F. W. Luscombe (A.B.); 29 A. W. Dunn (A.B.); 30, J. Fox (A.B.); 31, S. Patterson (A.B.); 32, T. W. Storey (A.B.); 33, J. T. Hicks (A.B.). Bottom row: 34, J. D. Armitage (A.B.); 35, E. M. Adams (1st P.O.); 36, A. E. C. Barrett (A.B.); 37, C. Williams (A.B.); 38, J. R. Wallwork (A.B.); 39, J. Healy (A.B.); 40, G. Robertson (leading seaman).

139

"B" COMPANY

Top row (reading from left to right): 1, A. H. Coppock (A.B.); 2, A. Smith (A.B.); 3 (——); 4, H. W. Fuller (A.B.); 5, J. Cooke (A.B.); 6, W. J. Jones (A.B.); 7, A. Ambrose (A.B.); 8, F. Sturch (A.B.); 9, J. Hurley (A.B.). Second row: 10, G. Clemson (A.B.); 11, C. J. Riddell (A.B.); 12, P. E. Wright (A.B.); 13, J. Dalby (A.B.); 14, G. Waite (A.B.); 15, C. A. Darcy (A.B.); 16, C. Bruton (A.B.); 17, H. Dugan (A.B.). Third row: 18, C. F. Burdett (2nd P.O.); 19, C. Nicholas (A.B.); 20, E. O'Connell (A.B.); 21, J. E. Woodcock; 22, D. Dadd (A.B.); 23, C. Murray (A.B.); 24, E. Fleming (A.B.); 25, C. Mathews (A.B.); 26, W. Walsh (A.B.); 27, Warrant-Officer J. Rolfe. Fourth row: 28, W. Hart (A.B.); 29, C. Bones (A.B.); 30, A. Share (A.B.); 31, H. Beale (A.B.); 32, T. D. Edmond (A.B.); 33, A. Murphy (A.B.); 34, A. Tate (A.B.); 35, E. T. Pittaway (A.B.); 36, C. Harder (A.B.); 37, W. H. Williams (A.B.). Bottom row: 38, R. W. H. Homer (leading seaman); 39, E. E. Watson (A.B.); 40, F. W. Pearse (signalman); 41, J. H. Brown (A.B.), 42, Bugler S. F. Freckleton; 43, T. Sayers (A.B.); 44, E. White (C.P.O.); 45, A. Geddes (A.B.); 46, E. T. Cane (1st P.O.); 47, W. Robison (A.B.); 48, A. Binkins (leading seaman); 49, A. Eves (A.B.).

THE AMBULANCE DETACHMENT.

Top row (reading from left to right): R. W. Hadden, A. E. M'Donald, C. A. M'Donald, W. Whitelaw, T. Armsby, A. Matthews, S. L. N. Harvison (dispenser), W. L. Maguire. Middle row: G. J. Sale, J. Gascoine, H. J. Atkinson (C.P.O.), H. Connor, J. T. Sippe, J. A. Blanchard. Bottom row: F. J. Pass, L. G. Field.

APPENDIX III

Victorian Contingent Nominal Roll

The lists of officers and men of the Victorian naval contingent who went to China in 1900 have been compiled from official records.

OFFICERS

Permanent Naval Forces
Commander .... F. Tickell
(Captain from 28 December 1900)
Lieutenant .... J. Biddlecombe
Gunner .... O.L.A. Burford
Gunner .... H.S. Claringbould
Gunner .... D.G. Inglis
Gunner .... R. Kearns
Gunner .... J. White
Staff Engineer .... W.G. Robertson
Paymaster .... A.M. Treacy
Staff Surgeon .... C.A. Stewart

Port Melbourne Division Naval Brigade
Chief Gunner .... E.G. Hayes
Gunner .... J.H. Marwood

Williamstown Division Naval Brigade
Gunner .... J.A. Bates
Gunner .... W. Hearn

RATINGS

Permanent Naval Forces

Stwd J.T. Adams
AB G.E. Aldridge
AB D. Barry
AB W.T. Bassett
Cook J.D. Beverley
LSMN A.H. Bury
AB A. Compton
AB B. Connell
AB H.W. Cooper
AB J. Cummings
AB A. Currer
Stoker W.M. Davis
AB J. Dorgan
AB J.W. Dunn
LSMN H. Farrington
PO1 M. Fitzpatrick
AB T. Francombe
Stoker W.M. Freeman
Boy A.A. Gibbs
PO1 T.W. Goding
AB D. Grant
AB E.E. Griffiths
AB F.W.V. Harris
AB M. Harty
Boy C.E. Holmes
Sigmn. W.H.J. Irons
AB F. Jackson
LStoker J.C. Jamieson
LSMN O. Jones
AB W.A. Kennedy
Cook W. Kirby
LSMN J.A. Lake
ERA A.J. Livingstone
AB J. Lyle
Stoker E. Lush
Stoker J. Mangan
AB J.M. McCarthy
CPO D.McDiarmid

AB A.B. McInnes
AB W. McIntosh
PO1 M. Mckenzie
PO1 D. McCleod
Stoker J. McNaughton
PO1 W.G. Monteith
PO1 T.E. Mooney
AB F.R. Morris
AB G. Morris
AB N. Morrison
Stoker G. Murdock
PO1 E.S. Mutton
AB A. Nugent
Cptr E. O'Brien
Stoker W. Parry
SBS W.S. Patchett
LSMN H. Petterson
AB G. Pilgrim
Ch.Arm. G. Prideaux
LSMN J. Roberts
AB A. Robertson
LSMN W. Robertson
AB T. Roche
Cptr. Mate W.M. Rogers
LStoker L. Salmon
Stoker P. Sheddon
LSMN P. Shenn
Stoker A. Sinclair
AB G. Stewart
AB H. Stonely
Stoker W.L. Sweetman
LSMN J. Thompson
AB J. Tyrell
ERA A.H. Vary
AB H. Waterman
Cptr. Mate J. Walker
Stwd J. White
AB E.L.J. Young

Port Melbourne Division Naval Brigade

AB J.F. Albon
Stoker J. Alexander
AB G. Alford
AB W.G. Allen

AB A.Anderson (1)
AB A. Anderson (2)
AB J. Bartlett
AB W.F. Bertotto

AB J.W. Brown
AB T. Carter
AB J. Charles
AB J. Coffey
AB W. Cole
AB E. Cooper
AB W. Crofts
AB C.H. Cunningham
AB A.T. Eastwood
AB G.H. Elkins
AB F. Ford
Stoker J.C. Ford
AB J. Foster
AB C.F. Fredricks
AB J. Gabriel
AB C.W. Gordon
Stoker R.B. Hamilton
PO2 R.J.B. Hampton
AB R.E. Hansen
AB G.J. Harding
AB C.W. Harvey
Bugler H. Hayes
AB L.M. Headford
AB J. Henwood
AB J.M. Hogg
AB J.E. Hughes
Stoker W. James
AB H. Kean
AB C.H. Kelson
AB P. Kennedy
Stoker R.G. Kenny
AB G.A. Laws

AB H.B. Lock
AB T. Lowry
AB D. McDonald
AB A. McKay
AB D. McPherson
AB J. Miller
PO2 A. Montague
AB J. Morgan
AB J. Muir
AB C. Nelson
AB R. Nicholls
Stoker C. Ogilvie
AB D.C. Pagan
AB W. Patterson
Stoker E. Pilling
AB J. Quinlan
AB G. Raeymackers
PO1 R. Reid
AB E. Roach
AB J. Scarsfield
AB A. Sharp
AB W. Slade
AB J. Smith
AB T.A. Smith
AB T.J. Smith
AB W.H. Stevens
AB J. Summerfield
AB T. Tonkin
AB G. Walters
AB T. Watson
AB A. Whiting
LSMN F.J. Young

Williamston Division Naval Brigade

AB G. Alexander
AB A. Anderson
AB J. Anderson
AB J.F. Andrew
AB W. Bates
AB F.W. Beaumont
AB W. Bryan
AC B.F. Churchill
AB G. D'Elton
AB E. Elso
PO2 J. Evans
AB H.W. Fletcher
AB G.A. Hale
PO2 R.B. Hansen

AB J. Hardy
AB F. Harris
AB C. Heffey
AB H. Henningsen
AB C.M. Honey
AB E. Hunter
AB J.E. Jamieson
AB T.R. Jones
AB F. King
AB W. Laing
AB J.A. McAllister
AB J. McConnell
AB A. McDonald
AB P. McGovern

The Victorian contingent which went to China in 1900 was paraded at the barracks at Williamstown, near Melbourne, for a 'photo call' before they embarked on board the troopship Salamis *to sail to Sydney to pick up their New South Wales colleagues. The drag ropes for the field guns they were to take with them as far as Hong Kong lie in the foreground. Unfortunately there is no key to the illustration.*

AB P. McKenzie
AB H. Mumford
AB W.C.F. Nagell
AB J. Nelson
AB C.E. Page
AB S.C. Peterson
AB S. Pike
AB M. Pope
AB W.H. Pope

AB W.F. Quaintin
AB S.J. Sheaf
AB A.G. Stephenson
AB J. Sylvester
PO1 W. Underwood
AB F.H. Wade
AB J. Wheelhouse
AB J. Wilson

ABBREVIATIONS

AB	Able Seaman	LSMN	Leading Seaman
CPO	Chief Petty Officer	PO1	Petty Officer 1st Class
Ch.Arm	Chief (Petty Officer) Armourer	PO2	Petty Officer 2nd Class
Cptr.	Carpenter	SBS	Sick Berth Steward
ERA	Engine Room Artificer	Sigmn	Signalman
LStoker	Leading Stoker	Stwd	(Officers) Steward

APPENDIX IV

Naval Contingents Personnel Statistics

THE VICTORIAN CONTINGENT

Death

Boy A.A. Gibbs (Capt. Tickell's servant). Died on board hospital ship *Carthage* on way to hospital at Wei-hai-wei. Buried at sea 19 October 1900.

Left behind in China

AB A. Anderson	left in hospital in Hong Kong; returned to Australia later
AB J. Harding	sword/sabre wounds rec'd in disturbance with Germans
AB Rasmussen	Joined Taku Tug & Lighterage Co. Took discharge in China

Invalided

AB J.F. Andrew	Arrived Australia March 1901
AB B. Bates	Arrived Australia March 1901
AB C.W. Gordon	Arrived Australia December 1900
AB M. Pope	Arrived Australia December 1900

Discipline

The only serious case recorded appears to have been that of Able Seaman J. Sylvester, who was sentenced to 90 days at hard labour in Hong Kong for abusive language to officers and who was invalided to Australia soon after he had served his sentence.

THE NEW SOUTH WALES CONTINGENT

Deaths

Staff Surgeon J. Steel	Peking
Able Seaman Eli Rose	Peking
Able Seaman A.J. Bennett	Peking
Able Seaman J. Hamilton	Tung-chao
Private T.J. Rogers	Tientsin
Private C.W. Smart	North Head, Sydney

Left Behind in China

AB T. Arnsby	hospital in Peking — enteric fever
Pte J.H. Ferns	hospital in Tientsin — German measles

Both men returned to Australia later.

The headstones of the graves of the three members of the New South Wales contingent who died in Peking and were buried in the cemetery near the British Legation there. Staff Surgeon Steele's grave is in the second row.

The following men accepted contracts for employment with the railway company. It is not known when they returned to Australia.

AB K.R. Bain	Pte H.G. Nixon
AB C. Boutell	LSMN A.E. Reed
AB E.A. Chambers	Pte F. Roberts
AB A. Denny	AB E. Ross
AB W.S. Graham	AB W. Thomas
Pte A. Harnett	AB W. Watts
Pte G.H. Johnson	AB W. Whiting
AB S. Miller	AB W.H. Williams
	AB W.J. Woods

Invalided to Australia

AB T. Conwell	November 1900
AB R. Conochie	December 1900
AB J. Hurley	October 1900
AB F. Leheman	December 1900
AB R.S. McGowan	October 1900
AB W.C. Milton	December 1900
AB A. Oliver	November 1900
AB W.H. Vine	November 1900
AB C.E. Whitely	October 1900

Discipline

As second-in-command of the New South Wales contingent, Commander Connor was responsible for the discipline of the men. Serious cases were dealt with by *punishment warrant*. A list of these warrants survives, and is included as a table to this Appendix. There is no record of more minor punishments given to the contingent. The incidence of drunkenness in the offences for which men were charged is noteworthy.

New South Wales Contingent — Warrant Punishments

Warrant No.	Date 1900	Rate Name	Charge	Punishment
1	7 Oct	AB Donachie R.	Mutinous language	90 days imprisonment (served in Hong Kong)
2	5 Nov	AB Giblin W.J.	Drunk, obscene & threatening language	7 days imprisonment
3	7 Nov	Pte McConnell J.	Willfully refusing duty	7 days imprisonment
4	1 Dec	LSMN Clemson G.	Drunk and disorderly	disrated (to AB), 7 days imprisonment
5	4 Dec	AB Wallwork J.B.	" "	7 days imprisonment
	1901			
6	2 Jan	AB Noble J.	Absent w/out leave & drunk	7 days imprisonment
7	14 Jan	AB Griffiths J.	Drunk and disorderly, insolent language	10 days imprisonment
8	24 Jan	AB Griffiths J.	Drunk, threatening language whilst a prisoner-at-large	42 days imprisonment
9	24 Jan	Sgt. Rogers R.	Drunk, creating disturbance in tent	disrated to corporal
10	21 Feb	PO Bennett A.J.	Drunk on duty, assaulting C.P.O. Sparkes	disrated to AB
11	21 Feb	LSMN Barnett J.	Improperly performing duties-allowing disturbance in room & not reporting same. Allowing trafficking	disrated to AB
12	13 Mar	AB Fleming E.	Drunk & assaulting Chinese in street	5 days imprisonment
13		No record		
14	2 Apr	LSMN Farley C.	Drunk & obscene language	disrated to AB
15	15 Apr	AB Thompson R.	Drunk & disobedience of orders	5 days cells

---

HMCS *PROTECTOR*

In marked contrast to the two naval brigade contingents the crew of the South Australian cruiser *Protector* had no deaths and no serious illness. The only major disciplinary problems seem to have concerned Mr Joss, the Warrant Boatswain, who was reprimanded on 3 October 1900 for 'improper conduct', a tantalising charge and one which is unfortunately not amplified, and Petty Officer Thomas Malloney, who was placed under arrest for being asleep on watch when the ship was in northern China and was replaced at his post by Petty Officer Perry, of flag-losing fame. There is no record of Malloney's punishment. Able Seaman Alfred Mackay missed the ship when she sailed from Sydney on 2 January 1901 on her way back to Adelaide and rejoined the ship there on 10 January.

APPENDIX V

HMCS *Protector* Technical Details

Type:	Steel-hulled cruiser.	Speed:	14.5 knots (design); 11+ knots (1900, sustained econ., w/sail assistance).
Builders:	Sir Wm Armstrong & Co., Newcastle-upon-Tyne, United Kingdom.		
		Bunkers:	150 tons coal
Displacement:	920 tons (555 Gross tonnage).	Feed Water:	30 tons each boiler, 30 tons general use
Length:	185 feet overall; 180 feet 6 inches between perpendiculars.		
		Endurance:	10 days at sustained speed w/sail assist.
Beam:	30 feet.		
Draught:	12 feet 6 inches.	Crew:	90−100 officers and men.
Machinery:	Two compound horizontal engines manufactured by Hawthorn Leslie. Scotch boilers.	Cost:	£65 000.
		Armament:	see Appendix VI.
		Armour:	1-inch steel belt on waterline.
Horsepower:	1500 I.H.P. total.		

General Description

The following description is taken from an account which appeared in the *Adelaide Advertiser* on the occasion of the ship's first arrival in the colony.

Protector's outward appearance is that of a low decked vessel built up several feet from the bow to right aft. She is divided into watertight compartments by 4 transverse bulkheads. The main deck is laid with teak planks 2½ inches thick. On the main deck are the galleys, officers quarters and principal steering gear. The Captain's cabin is on the lower deck, there being an entrance to it, aft, just in front of the stern gun. It is upholstered in Morocco, the woodwork being of mahogany.

Crews quarters are on the lower deck forward. Magazines are on the main deck, one fore and one aft. They are built of steel plates lined with lead so as to be perfectly watertight.

Above the main deck, extending from about amidships to the low forward deck, is a square hurricane deck, on which is fixed a conning tower formed of inch steel plates. It contains steering wheels, with speaking tubes to various parts of the vessel, as well as chart tables and boxes.

APPENDIX VI

HMCS *Protector* Armament Details

 Altohugh HMCS *Protector* underwent many changes to her armament in her long career, in 1900 she was armed almost identically with the equipment she had when she was built in 1884.

The ship was extremely heavily armed for her size, with the general layout of her guns as shown in the diagram. The largest weapon was an 8-inch bow chaser. This rifled breech-loading Woolwich-Armstrong gun was mounted on an Elswick naval carriage and slide. It was carried in the forward part of the superstructure on the hurricane deck.

The gun weighed 12 tons and the carriage 7½ tons. There was stowage on board for 50 projectiles. Shells were of four types — chilled, common, segment and shrapnel. Their average weight was about 180 lbs. A Full charge of propellant was 100 lb of prismatic powder contained in two cartridges.

A Reduced charge of propellant was 65 lbs of pebble powder in two cartridges.

The range of the gun using a Full charge was about 7500 yards. Muzzle velocity at Full charge was 2030 feet per second (f.p.s.).

A crew of between ten and thirteen men was required to serve the mounting.

Protector's secondary armament consisted of 6-inch guns. These were breech-loading weapons on Vavasseur central pivot mountings. Two

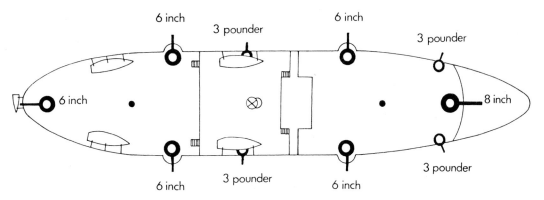

Diagram of the armament of the South Australian Navy's cruiser HMCS Protector *as it was in 1900 when the ship went to China as part of the Australian colonial force sent to assist in suppressing the Boxer uprising.*

All that remains in 1984 of the 8-inch gun removed from the South Australian warship HMCS Protector and mounted on shore near Adelaide.

6-inch gun from HMCS Protector mounted on shore after having been removed from the ship before World War I and photographed in 1984.

guns were mounted on each beam in casemates in the superstructure and one at the stern with a 1-inch steel shield. They varied very slightly in minor detail.

The guns were built by Woolwich-Armstrong at Elswick. The gun weighed 5 tons and the carriage, less shield, another 5½ tons.

Three types of shell were carried — common, chilled and shrapnel. Each weighed about 80 lbs. There was stowage on board for 50 projectiles for each gun.

A Full charge consisted of between 42 and 50 lbs of cocoa prismatic powder, and a Reduced charge was 30 lbs of pebble powder.

The Full charge range of the gun was about 7200 yards. The muzzle velocity was between 1840 and 2060 f.p.s., depending on the model of the gun.

A crew of between five to eight men was required for each gun.

Protector was also armed with small Quick-Firing (Q.F.) guns to engage fast torpedo boats.

The term 'quick-firing' was used to describe a gun which employed the then newly introduced long-recoil system which allowed a much higher rate of fire than had been possible before. It also made possible the introduction of 'fixed' ammunition where the shell and propellant charge were joined together in the same way as a rifle bullet rather than the two parts being separate, as had been the case previously.

Four Hotchkiss 3-pounder guns were sited on the hurricane deck amidships, near the funnel. As their name suggests, they fired a 3 lb projectile, which was about 1½ inches in diameter. Ammunition was fixed. The gun weighed ¼ ton and the mounting a little more. It was

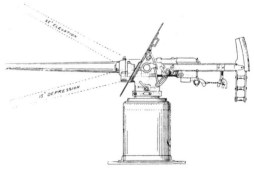

Drawing of the 3-pounder Hotchkiss quick-firing gun as fitted to HMCS Protector.

loaded through a rising breech and the recoil was absorbed by a spring and hydraulic cylinder which was mercury filled. A system of manual firing was used. H-type sights were graduated to 3400 yards, and the speed scale on the tangent sight was graduated to 30 knots each way. A 6x telescope was fitted.

Gatling guns may have been mounted when the ship went to China, although this is not certain. Five guns may have been carried. Each gun had ten barrels of 0.45 inch. Each barrel had its own lock. The gun weighed 230 lbs and the mounting 40 lb. The rate of fire was 1200 r.p.m per mounting. It is thought that 10 000 rounds were carried on board.

We do not know how much ammunition *Protector* took on board when she went to China, but there is a partial record of what was returned to the stores on the ship's return to Adelaide.

8″ Full charges	7 cases,	10	charges
Reduced ″	21 ″	38 ½	″
6″ Full charges	8 ″	48	charges
Reduced ″	41 ″	245	″

6″ shell, common, filled		75
″ ″ empty		25
6″ ″ shrapnel, filled		40
6″ ″ chilled, ″		27

Fuses (time, mechanical)   320

36 Martini-Henry rifles with all accoutrements
38 revolvers, Webley

APPENDIX VII

Naval Contingents — Details of Small Arms and Artillery

(Section on small arms contributed by the Antique Arms Collectors Society of Australia.)

THE Victorian contingent left Australia with Martini-Enfield Mk II rifles. This rifle was converted from the Martini-Henry rifle which had been introduced into service in 1876. The conversion gave the rifle a calibre of .303 inches with 5-groove Enfield rifling with a left-hand twist. The overall length of the rifle was 46.5 inches with a barrel length of 30.2 inches. The conversion pattern was sealed in February 1896.

The bayonet for the rifle was the Pattern 1895 with a triangular blade 21.5 inches long. This was converted from the Pattern 1876 bayonet for the Martini-Henry. When fixed to the rifle it was sited below the barrel as opposed to on the right hand side.

When the Victorians reached Hong Kong they exchanged their rifles for the then newest design available from Imperial sources. This was the Magazine Lee-Metford Rifle Mk II*.

This rifle was of .303 calibre with 7-groove Metford rifling with a left-hand twist. Its overall length was 49.5 inches with a barrel length of 30.2 inches. The magazine held ten rounds of ammunition. The only difference between the Mk II* and the Mk II was the addition of a safety catch on the cocking piece. This modification was approved on 22 April 1895. The rifle was manufactured in small numbers by the ordnance factories at Enfield and Sparkbrook.

The Martini-Enfield Mk II rifle.

*The Lee-Metford Rifle Mk II**

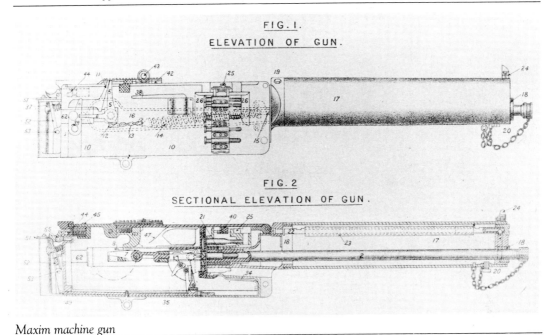

Maxim machine gun

The New South Wales contingent carried Lee-Metford Mk II rifles throughout their deployment to China. The weapon was a predecessor of the Lee-Metford Mk II*, and was similar in appearance. The rifles had been drawn from Royal Navy ordnance stocks on Spectacle Island in Sydney harbour.

Officers and Chief and Petty Officers of both contingents were armed with revolvers. A few of the Victorian contingent carried the Enfield Mk I revolver. This weapon had been accepted into service on 10 August 1880. It was a 6-shot self-extracting revolver of .476 calibre and a barrel length of 6 inches. It was a cumbersome weapon to use and reload and was almost universally loathed by troops.

The Webley Mk I revolver was a .455 calibre 6-shot revolver with a 4-inch barrel. It was accepted as a standard weapon for the British armed forces on 18 July 1897. Its patent had been sealed on 8 November 1887 and approved on 2 February 1892.

Both contingents were issued with the Maxim machine gun in Hong Kong on their

The Enfield revolver

The Webley revolver

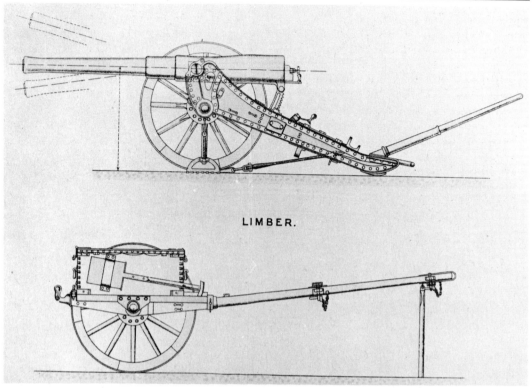

LIMBER.

12-pounder field gun — standard version

12-pounder field gun with New South Wales contingent, Peking 1901.

way to China. It was produced for the British armed forces in two calibres, .303 and .45. The contingents were issued with the latter model.

The gun was a water-cooled weapon with a rate of fire of 70 rounds per minute (rpm) in deliberate fire or 450 rpm in rapid fire. Sights were calibrated up to 2900 yards, with battle sights set to 3, 4, or 500 yards. The weapon weighed 60 lbs without a mounting, of which there were various models. Cartridges were normally supplied in belts of 84 rounds.

The Nordenfeldt gun which the Victorians had brought with them from Australia is illustrated on page 30. It had five barrels of rifle calibre fixed side-by-side and was actuated by a lever working backwards and forwards. It was capable of firing either volleys or single rounds. According to a contemporary account '. . . the mechanism is simple and strong and the action very reliable at 600 rpm'.

Both contingents were equipped with the Royal Navy's 12-pounder, 12 hundredweight (cwt) field gun. Two versions are illustrated — the diagram illustrates the general-purpose version and the photograph shows the New South Wales contingent with one of the versions they had in Peking. The only difference appears to be in the carriage.

The gun itself, when complete with carriage and limber, weighed 27 cwt or almost 1½ tons. The bore of the gun was 3 inches, and the rifling had 16 grooves. It could be fired either electrically or by percussion. Ammunition was separate, with a 3 lb charge firing a 12 lb projectile for a range of up to 5600 yards.

The limber held 12 projectiles and 12 cartridges, which meant that care had to be taken with the expenditure of ammunition.

APPENDIX VIII

Medals Awarded

(Contributed by James J. Atkinson)

Two medals of interest are associated with the Boxer uprising.

CHINA WAR MEDAL — 1900

Officers and men of both contingents who served in north China with the China Field Force and the ship's company of HMCS/HMS *Protector* received the Queen's China Medal without clasp.

The issue had been sanctioned by Queen Victoria before her death in early 1901 and was confirmed by His Majesty King Edward VII on 3 January 1902.

The 36 mm diameter silver medal hangs by a straight swivelling suspender from a 33 mm wide ribbon of crimson with yellow edges. The obverse shows the crowned and veiled head of Queen Victoria and the legend 'Victoria Regina Et Imperatrix'.

The reverse depicts a shield bearing the Royal Arms, surrounded by a number of weapons, a cannon, an anchor and a capstan, all under a palm tree, around which is the motto 'Armis Exposcere Pacem' (Peace maintained by force of arms), whilst the title 'China 1900' is in the exergue.

THE MILITARY ORDER OF THE DRAGON

Officers of the three colonies were also eligible for membership in the 'Military Order of the Dragon', a private order founded on 1 October 1900 in the Imperial Palace in Peking by a group of officers representing the various nations who participated in suppressing the Boxer uprising. The formation of the order was the initiative of some American officers, and officers of Allied countries were given honorary membership. *Qualifications for Membership* were:

Active. All regular and volunteer commissioned officers in the United States Army, Navy, Marine Corps, Acting Assistant Surgeons and authorised Volunteer Staff Officers who served as such, or as an enlisted man in northern

China or in the Gulf of Pechihli in connection with or as part of any military operation and under the orders of the respective Army or Navy commander thereof, between 15 June and 31 December 1900 and all members of the Diplomatic and Consular Corps of the United States in Tientsin and Peking during the said period, were eligible for active membership.

Hereditary. The nearest male descendant, twenty-one years of age or older, of Active members could become Hereditary members upon election by the Executive Committee and payment of the requisite fees and dues. Upon the death of the Active member from whom the Hereditary member derived eligibility, such Hereditary member would become an Active member and transferred to the active list.

Honorary. All members of the foreign diplomatic corps present on duty at any time during the period 15 June to 31 December 1900; all military and naval commissioned officers of other services than that of the United States

present in northern China or in the Gulf of Pechihli, and engaged in military operations thereat, between the dates shown above, may become Honorary members.

Chancellery of the Order was at Governor's Island, New York.

The first President of the Order, until his death in 1914, was Major General Adna Romanza Chaffee, United States Army, who was the commander of the American 'China Relief Expeditions'.

Apart from the Americans the Order contained Honorary members from the United Kingdom, France, Germany, Italy, and Russia. A number of officers from the New South Wales contingent joined the Order, but, despite eligibility, none joined from Victoria or South Australia.

Upon election a member was required to forward $10.00 to Bailey, Banks & Biddle Co., Jewellers of Philadelphia, the makers of the insignia of the Order.

Lieut Staunton Spain's Military Order of the Dragon — an American 'private' order

Medals awarded to Midshipman C.E. Murnin of the New South Wales Naval Brigade for service in China 1900–1901.

PHOTOGRAPH CREDITS

Numbers refer to page numbers.

Permission to use the photographs in this book has been given by the following individuals & organisations, with whom the copyright, where applicable, remains.

Australian War Memorial.
Front end paper, (AWM 19821), 4(bottom right)(A5056), 14(top)(AWM19863), 16(top) (Naval Collection), 18(Naval Collection), 20(AWM19865), 25(AWM 300009), 30(top) (AWM19854), 30(bottom)(A4476), 32(A4808), 43(A5978), 44(Naval Collection), 45(Naval Collection), 49(A5042), 57(top) (A4475), 66(A5032), 75(left)(A5041), 76(top)(A4483), 89(A4935), 91(A5047), 94(bottom right)(A5023), 95(top)(A5070), 96(A4480), 102(A5059), 104(A5114), 105(A5026), 107(A5035), 109(A106037), 110(A4488), 119(A5058), 121(top)(A5058) (bottom)(A5050), 125(bottom)(A5061), 128(top right), 129(A5054), 154(bottom) (A5049).

Mitchell Library, State Library of New South Wales.
46, 48(top), 53, 54, 70(bottom left), 85, 95(bottom left & right), 108, 112, 114(top), 122, 125(top), 128(bottom right), 130(top), 130(bottom), 131, 146.

State Library of New South Wales.
23(lower), 26, 35, 39, 47(top), 47(bottom left), 48(bottom right), 71(top), 76(bottom), 83, 86, 97, 103, 135, 138–140, 144.

National Library of Australia.
12, 15, 16(bottom left), 19, 21.

BBC Hulton Picture Library.
9(left), 9(right), 61(top).

South Australian Dept. Education.
149

South Australian State Archives.
37, 50.

New South Wales Parliament.
24.

Oberlin College.
7.

Royal Australian Navy.
13, 17, 132.

Wardroom Mess, HMAS Penguin.
23(top), 128(top left).

The Naval Historical Society of Australia.
19(top).

United Service Institution of New South Wales.
3, 4(top), 8, 11, 27, 31, 56, 59, 67, 74, 120, 153.

J. Atkinson.
70(top), 116, 119, 126, 128(bottom left), 133, 158(4 photos).

J. Nicholls.
150(top left), 150(bottom left).

Chris Hall.
14(bottom right), 38, 79, 80, 82.

Antique Arms Collectors Society of Australia.
152(top), 152(bottom), 153(bottom left), 153(bottom right).

Private Collections.
34, 57(bottom right), 61(bottom left), 69(4 photos), 71(bottom), 75(right), 87, 88, 94(top), 99, 113, 127, 150(bottom right), 154(top), 157.

BIBLIOGRAPHY

Atkinson, James J. *Australian Contingents to the China Field Force 1900–1901*, New South Wales Military Historical Society, Sydney, 1976

Blake, W. *Adventures of a Naval Chief Gunner* Brisbane: 1906

Department of Defence (Navy), An Outline of Australian Naval History Canberra: Australian Government Publishing Service, 1976

Field, L.M. *The Forgotten War* Melbourne: Melbourne University Press, 1979

Fleming, Peter *The Siege at Peking* Hong Kong: Oxford University Press, 1983

Gillett, Ross *Australia's Colonial Navies* Sydney: Naval Historical Society of Australia, 1982

—— *Australian and New Zealand Warships 1914–1945* Sydney: Doubleday, 1983

Macandie, G.L. *The Genesis of the R.A.N.* Sydney: Government Printer, 1949

Morris, James *Heaven's Command* London: Faber & Faber, 1973

—— *Farewell the Trumpets*, London: Faber & Faber, 1978

Odgers, George *The Royal Australian Navy — An Illustrated History* Sydney: Child & Henry, 1982.

Warner, Marina *The Dragon Empress* London: Weidenfeld & Nicolson, 1972

Watts, Anthony J. *Pictorial History of the Royal Navy* London: vol. two, 1880–1914 Ian Allen, 1971

Wedd, Monty *Australian Military Uniforms 1800–1982* Sydney: Kangaroo Press, 1982

NEWSPAPERS

Sydney Morning Herald
Daily Telegraph (Sydney)
Age (Melbourne)

Adelaide Observer
Australian Town and Country Journal

MANUSCRIPT SOURCES

Australian War Memorial, Canberra.
War in China, 1900–1901
   Sergeant-Major B. Blyth's Collection
     3 DRL 2181

Personal Records of McCarthy, Joseph M.
   3 DRL 3068
Personal Records of Lofts, H.E.
   3 DRL 2180

Personal Records of Jeffery, George F.
3 DRL 2246
The Victorian Naval Contingent to China,
1900. AWM1 Item 64

'Imperialists' and 'policemen'?: the Australians
in China 1900–1901, Robyn McWhinney.
BA thesis, Macquarie University 1974.
AWM 422/3/154

PRIVATE COLLECTIONS

Diary — William Bertotto
Diary — Cecil E. Murnin
Diary — Edward R. Connor

INDEX